Unforgettable
Helen
A Motion Picture script for reading

Written By

Phillips Wylly.

Unforgettable Helen WGA 1867742   Phillips Wylly

This is the original manuscript as formatted by the author, Phillips Wylly.

"Unforgettable Helen, A Motion Picture script for reading," by Phillips Wylly. ISBN 978-1-949756-23-4 (Softcover); 978-1-949756-24-1 (Hardcover).

Published 2019 by Virtualbookworm.com Publishing Inc., P.O. Box 9949, College Station, TX 77842, US.

©2019, Phillips Wylly. All rights reserved. No part of this publication may be reproduced, stored in a retrieval system, or transmitted in any form or by any means, electronic, mechanical, recording or otherwise, without the prior written permission of Phillips Wylly.

Unforgettable Helen WGA 1867742   Phillips Wylly

Author's note:

This is the story of Helen Fogel.
When Helen was seventeen years old she was told her name was "Too Jewish," and she became Helen Forrest. Over the next few years she was several times Billboard Magazine's Number One "Fem Singer" as she stared with Artie Shaw, Benny Goodman and Harry James. Names familiar to us "old folk," names probably unknown to most folk.

I met Helen long after her starring years and learned of her remarkable life. She and I talked about a motion picture. Why I did not follow up on that idea then I do not know, but now, at last, the script is complete.
Today's production companies do not believe Helen's story will make a viable film. There are no car chases, no multiple shootings, no space monsters. So be it. But for any of you who may wish to venture into Helen's world I urge you to find some of her recordings on the internet or CD's available at Amazon. Listen a little, watch a little then come meet this wonderful lady.

Unforgettable Helen WGA 1867742   Phillips Wylly

FADE IN:

A 1930s radio fills the screen.
              RADIO ANNOUNCER VOICE OVER
       For your listening pleasure it's the music of
              Eddie Duchin and his Orchestra
       Music up: Cole Porter's "Night and Day"

Note: It is intended that all songs and music be original recordings by indicated artists

Fade In Title superimposed over 1930 style table top radio:

A

MEMORY

PRODUCTION

DISSOLVE:

Unforgettable Helen WGA 1867742   Phillips Wylly

EXTERIOR (EXT).   BEAUTIFUL LEAFY TREES
   Music continues as vocal begins   Then, in sync with lyric

Night and Day,
You are the one...

ZOOM IN MAIN TITLE OVER TREE BACKGROUND:

Unforgettable
Helen

FADE OUT MAIN TITLE
   Music continues.

FADE IN NEW TITLE   OVER LEAFY TREE BACKGROUND

The story of a Forrest called Trees

Music and Lyrics continue then at 2nd chorus lyric
   DAY AND <u>NIGHT</u>

FAST CUT TO:

Unforgettable Helen WGA 1867742   Phillips Wylly

EXT - NIGHT. NOW BLACK & WHITE FILM (B&W)
CLOCK ON NY TIMES BUILDING
.   Snowflakes in the cold air.   We hear tower clock bell
           begin ringing as clock tells us the time is 5:00

EXT - B&W - EVENING AERIAL VIEW OF MANHATTAN
LIGHTS.
           Eddie Duchin music and clock tower bell continue
           Camera slowly moves to the East River and on to
           Brooklyn.

EXT: B&W AERIAL
           Camera slowly angles down to view of residential street
           of modest homes and then focuses on a single house.

           SUPER IMPOSE : "NOVEMBER 1934' BOTTOM OF SCREEN

INTERIOR (INT.) B&W - KITCHEN - NIGHT. CLOSE UP (CU)
RADIO (Same radio as in Main Title.)
           As Duchin music continues, Camera slowly pulls back to reveal
           scruffy looking 40 or so year old man, wearing an undershirt, seated
           at the kitchen table nursing a shot glass half full of whiskey as a
           sixteen year old girl, back to him, carries tray holding dinner left
           overs to the ice box. She is softly humming Duchin music.

INT. B&W - MEDIUM CLOSE UP (MCU)   REAR OF GIRL AT ICE
BOX

INT. B&W - KITCHEN   MCU SCRUFFY MAN
           As he takes a sip of booze and obviously enjoys what he is looking at.

Unforgettable Helen WGA 1867742   Phillips Wylly

NT. B&W - KITCHEN ICE BOX
    Girl opens the top door of a 1920s ice box. An ice cake in the top compartment provides the chill.) Still humming softly Girl puts something in ice chest, closes that door then opens the lower door and puts other left overs in box below..

INT, B&W KITCHEN MS. (Medium Shot) SCRUFFY MAN SEATED AT TABLE AS GIRL RETURNS TO COLLECT MORE DIRTY DISHES.
    Standing just to his side she bends to pick up a plate and a kitchen knife. As she does the man quickly downs what's left of his drink, grabs her and pulls her onto his lap with one arm while he reaches for her blouse with the other.

INT. B&W - KITCHEN MS MAN AND GIRL (Music Out)
    Startled, surprised, terrified, The girl slashes at his hand with the knife she is holding and tries to pull away. No need to pull away. The man dumps her on to the floor and grabs his bleeding hand.

                    MAN (shouting0
                    You Bitch!

Scrambling to her feet girl dashes to the kitchen door, opens it, throws knife to the floor and runs out into the night.

INT. B&W - KITCHEN. EVENING
    Woman wearing tired looking negligee comes dashing into the kitchen.
                    WOMAN
                What happened?
                    MAN
(Holding up his bleeding hand.)
    Your fuckin' god damn daughter cut me. That bitch!!

EXT. B&W MLS (High angle Long Shot) RESIDENTIAL STREET - Almost no traffic. Perhaps a horse drawn trolley car in the distance as the terrified girl, trying not to slip on patches of ice, runs from the house. Looking back over her shoulder in fear of pursuit she is unaware of the car that almost hits her as she crosses an intersection.

Unforgettable Helen WGA 1867742   Phillips Wylly

EXT. B&W - ROW HOUSE - NIGHT
    Here there may be safety. Three steps up from the sidewalk then a short cement path to three more steps up onto the front porch.

CU. B&W- FRONT DOOR BELL
    A small sign above the bell proclaims: H. SILVERMAN. PIANO LESSONS.

EXT B&W FRONT DOOR MCU
    Pounding on the door with one hand the terrified girl presses the doorbell with the other as she sobs,

                  GIRL
            Help. Help me.

EXT B&W MS FRONT DOOR OPENS.
    A pleasant looking woman - perhaps 40, 45 , opens the door. She is Honey Silverman
                  HONEY
           (In great surprise)
    Helen! Oh my god, what's happened to you?

Helen virtually   throws herself into woman's arms.

                HELEN (sobbing)
      Please Don't let him get me… Oh please.

EXT TO INT. B&W SILVERMAN FRONT ENTRANCE
    Honey Silverman puts her arms around the terrified girl and leads her into the house.

INT   B&W SILVERMAN HOUSE
    Honey Silverman half carries, half leads Helen towards a comfortable looking sofa in the living room.

                  HONEY
       It's alright. It's alright Helen.
       You're safe here.

Unforgettable Helen WGA 1867742   Phillips Wylly

INT. B&W SILVERMAN HOUSE LIVING ROOM AND STAIRWAY TO SECOND FLOOR.
A man wearing tuxedo trousers but only an undershirt and with shaving cream on half his face comes dashing down the stairs. He is Jerome Silverman, Honey's husband.

                        JEROME
                What's up? What's goin' on?

As Honey helps Helen onto the couch as she gestures "calm down" to her husband
                        HONEY
It's alright. It's Helen.   She's had a little trouble at home. Check the front door make sure it's locked. Then maybe you could get her a glass of warm milk.

                        JEROME
                  Yeah, Yeah sure....

He checks the front door, locks it then turns and heads for the kitchen.

INT. B&W SILVERMAN KITCHEN
Jerome heads for the ice box, takes out a real 1930's milk bottle with cream at the top. He shakes bottle to mix in cream, finds a pot, pours milk into it. Lights stove with a match, puts the pot on and goes to find a glass.

INT. B&W SILVERMAN LIVING ROOM.
Helen with her head on Honey's shoulder and Honey's arm around her, She is more calm now as Jerome, carrying the requested glass of warm milk, enters the room.

                        HONEY (Takes milk, looks at Jerome)
            It was her stepfather. He tried.... You know.

                        JEROME (shakes his head in disgust)
                  Jesus....

> HONEY (to Jerome)
> Now you hurry up. don't be late.

> JEROME
> I don't think I should leave you all
> alone here tonight.

> HONEY
> Oh we're fine now. You get out of here
> and leave us girls alone.

> JEROME (As he heads for the stairs)
> You sure?

> HONEY.
> Yes. Now beat it.

Jerome gives a nod then takes the stairs two at a time as he heads back to the bathroom and the rest of his clothing.

INT. B&W MCU HELEN AND HONEY
Helen and Honey seated on couch. Honey holds glass to Helen's lips

> HELEN
> Thank you (a murmur as she take glass)
> (She sips milk) Oooo. Hot.

> HONEY
> Should have warned you. He doesn't
> know the meaning of warm. Let it cool
> a minute

Helen tries to smile as she blows on the milk then takes another sip

> HELEN (nodding)
> Umm, that's better. Thank you.

Unforgettable Helen WGA 1867742   Phillips Wylly

> HONEY
> Good. Now you stay in our guest
> room tonight and tomorrow we'll get
> all this straightened out.

INT. B&W NEW ANGLE LIVING ROOM INCLUDING STAIRS
As Jerome, now dressed with a bow tie and jacket, comes down the stairs. He looks to Helen and his wife.

> JEROME
> Honey, you sure you will be alright?

INT. B&W CU HONEY

> HONEY
> Absolutely. Just make sure the door's locked
> and get going. You don't want to be late
> on a new job.

INT. B&W LIVING ROOM MS JEROME AT FRONT DOOR

> JEROME.
> Okay.

Jerome out door. But only a second later he is back in to pick up a sheaf of music from the hall table.

> JEROME
> Might need the music.

And then he is gone.

INT. B&W LIVING ROOM - MCU HELEN AND HONEY ON COUCH
Honey with her arm around Helen who is comfortable now.

> HONEY
> You know, I have been thinking...

Unforgettable Helen WGA 1867742   Phillips Wylly

INT, B&W CU HELEN
Helen looks questioningly at Honey

                        HELEN
                        Yesss???

INT B&W MCU HELEN AND HONEY

                        HONEY
    I think it's about time to let him in on our secret.

EXT. B&W RESIDENTIAL STREET - DAY
Honey and Jerome Silverman walking purposefully up the street

                        HONEY
        I'm glad you could come with me,
        I wouldn't want to talk to them alone.

                        JEROME
        I certainly wouldn't let you go alone.
        The father must be a real son-of-a-itch.

                        HONEY
        Jerome. Such language. And he isn't
        her father, he's her Step-Father.

EXT.. B&W HELEN'S HOUSE - DAY
Jerome and Honey reach the walkway leading to three steps up to the front porch of a house similar to their own. They climb the steps and ring front door bell.

EXT. - B&W FRONT DOOR - DAY.
Door opens to reveal, still in an undershirt, Helen's Step-Father.

                        STEP-FATHER
        Yeah, what-a ya want.

                    HONEY
            I'm Mrs. Silverman. May I speak with
            Helen's mother please.

                    STEP-FATHER
            Yeah. Wait a minute.

Almost before his words are out, still wearing the same negligee she wore last night,, Helen's mother appears. She looks rather blankly at Honey.

                    HONEY
            I'm Mrs. Silverman

                    HELEN'S MOTHER
            I know who you are...

                    HONEY
            Your daughter stayed with us last night.
            She told us what happened. She does
            not want to come back.

Before Helen's mother can speak up the Step-Father jumps in

                    STEP-FATHER
            And we sure don't want the little bitch back!

                    HONEY
            That's fine. She can live with us.
            Her room and board will be five dollars a week.
            And that will be in addition to the twenty-five
            cents a week for her music lessons. Due every
            Friday. We'll pick up her things tomorrow.

EXT DAY. B&W FRONT PORCH AND STEPS
Before following his wife as she starts away, Jerome looks directly at the Step-Father.

JEROME
We don't want trouble from you. You show up at our house we call the police and tell 'em everything that's happened.

Jerome turns away and joins Honey. He does not see

EXT B&W FRONT PORCH CU STEP FATHER GIVES F--- YOU GESTURE

EXT B&W STREET
Jerome and Honey walking back to their house.

JEROME
I'm glad to have her with us but I'm not sure five dollars a week is enough....

HONEY
With half of what you'll be paying her it should be plenty.

JEROME (surprise on his face)
What? I pay her? Why am I gone Pay her?

HONEY
Well you pay every body in your orchestra.

EXT STREET. B&W MCU JEROME STOPS WALKING TAKES HONEY'S ARM AND TURNS HER TO FACE HIM.

JEROME
Honey doll, Honey baby,, Honey pie. I got news for you. I already got a piano player. Me.

                    HONEY
Oh she's not gonna play piano. We haven't really been
working on the piano for a long time. What she can really
do is sing. We were going to surprise you one day. So this
is the day. She's the singer you been looking for..

With that Honey turns and continues walking down the street.

EXT STREET. B&W   CU JEROME. HALF LAUGHING AS HE SHAKES HIS HEAD
                    JEROME
                    Oh my…

INT.: CU FOOT WORKING PEDDLE ON SEWING MACHINE
Camera pulls back to reveal The Silverman bedroom turned into a
temporary costume shop. Helen, wearing a slip, stands watching
Mrs. S. working at the foot peddle sewing machine. She is stitching
the hem of what we will soon discover is a full length evening gown.
Hem completed, Honey stands to help Helen put it on as off camera
voice is heard:

                    JEROME (Voice over)
         (Not exactly a shout but in a tone we will remember)
                    Helen!

INTERIOR. B&W FOOT OF STAIRS SILVERMAN HOUSE
Standing at the foot of the stairs, wearing an overcoat over his
orchestra uniform, holding a coat for Helen and glancing impatiently
at his watch, Jerome continues

                    JEROME
         Honey. Helen. Come on. We got-a go.

Unforgettable Helen WGA 1867742   Phillips Wylly

INT. TOP OF STAIRS - AND NOW WE GO FROM B&W TO FULL COLOR
    As we hear Leo Reisman's Hit recording of Cole Porter's "You've Got That Thing." In sync with vocal:
        "You've got that thing,
          That certain ting…"
    Fully dressed, Helen appears at the head of the stairs. Music swells;

INT. - FULL COLOR   JEROME AT FOOT OF STAIRS. (Music continues)
    A wide smile on Jerome's face as he watches Helen descend.

              JEROME
       Oh my goodness. What a beautiful lady!

    Music out

INT. FULL COLOR   CU SUBWAY TYPE TURN STYLE   Jerome's hand slips a nickel into the ancient turn style.
    Camera widens as Helen pushes through and Jerome adds another nickel for himself then follows her.

EXT. ELEVATED TRAIN STATION PLATFORM.
    Helen and Jerome join the crowd waiting for the "El." It is only a moment before a train pulls into the station and they rush to find seats, there are none. They grab strap hangers as train jolts away.

EXT. LS - EL TRAIN ON BROOKLYN BRIDGE -
    From almost any location on the Brooklyn Bridge the view of down town Manhattan is wondrous but at probably no other time of day is it quite so spectacular as early evening when the city lights are coming on and there is still enough daylight to outline the massive skyscrapers.

Unforgettable Helen WGA 1867742   Phillips Wylly

INT. EL TRAIN (Music down and out.)
    Hanging on to the strap Helen bends so that she can see through the train's windows.

                      HELEN (almost whispering)
                It's beautiful...

                      JEROME (watching he)
        Being able to see that almost makes living in
        Brooklyn worthwhile doesn't it.

    Helen is too mesmerized by the beauty to respond

EXT. EL TRAIN LEAVING BRIDGE. (FULL COLOR NOW UNTIL END OF SCRIPT)

INT. EL TRAIN
    With the spectacular view now replaced by the walls of buildings lining the Third Avenue El's tracks Helen straightens up, shaking her head in an expression of wonderment and delight she takes a deep breath then turns to Mr. Silverman.

                      HELEN
        Mister Silverman, what's a Dance-a-thon?

                      JEROME
        I guess you'd call it an endurance contest really.
        Starts with a lot of couples dancing twenty-four hours
        a day. One by one they get exhausted and stop.
        Last couple left wins the prize.

                      HELEN (a bit surprised)
        Gee. What's the prize?

                      JEROME
        I guess different contests have different prizes.
        This one is a hundred dollars.

Unforgettable Helen WGA 1867742   Phillips Wylly

INT. TRAIN CU HELEN
Helen is stunned $100 is more money than she has ever seen.

                    HELEN
        A hundred dollars! Wow.
        Why do I wanna sing?
        Let me get a partner and dance.

EXT. NIGHT EL TRAIN STAIRS LEADING DOWN TO
3rd AVE. SIDEWALK.
Helen and Jerome make their way down the steps then start along the sidewalk towards the distant arena marquee.

EXT NIGHT - CU MARQUE: "DANCE-A-THON TONIGHT"

INT. ARENA.
Jerome and Helen walk through tunnel leading to the grandstands. As they emerge Helen is wide eyed at what she sees: A modest crowd of seated spectators watching the twenty or so tired looking couples not exactly dancing but moving around the floor somewhat in time to Duke Ellington's "Sophisticated Lady." Each man has a number on his back.

INT. ARENA NEW ANGLE
As Helen and Jerome approach the platform overlooking the dance floor the recorded music ends and Helen can see a man moving away from the turntable then stepping to a microphone.

INT. ARENA MCU MAN AT MICROPHONE

                MAN AT MIKE
        Okay dancers, it's break time. Fifteen minutes rest.
        Then we're back with the live music of
        Gerry Mann and his orchestra..

INT ARENA. ANGLE ON HELEN AND JEROME
Approaching the platform where orchestra members are setting up

                    HELEN
                Gerry Mann???

                    JEROME
                Yeah. That's my working name.

(After a pause, as they step onto the platform, Jerome continues)

                    JEROME
              I didn't think... Your name, Fogel? Isn't it? Helen Fogel?

                    HELEN
                Yes...

                    JEROME
              Umm...Like mine, too Jewish. Let' see... how about Forrest. We can spell it with two R's. That'll make it special. Come on I'll introduce you to Red.

INT ARENA CU HELEN
Helen shakes her head as Jerome leads her to the MC. It is all too much. This huge arena (It isn't that big, kind of small as arenas go but Helen has never been in one before.) The dancers. The orchestra. Helen Forrest with two R's....

INTERIOR ARENA - MC "RED" HELEN AND JEROME

                    MC "RED"
              High Gerry. Who's this beautiful lady?

GERRY/JEROME
She's our new vocalist Red. Helen Forrest.
That's Forrest with two "R's"
(turning to Helen)
Helen, say hello to our boss, Red Skelton.

HELEN
Hello Mr. Skelton

RED SKELTON
Hi Helen with two R's.

As Helen accepts Red's hand shake, Red turns to Gerry Mann.

RED SKELTON
Almost time, we're back in five.

GERRY / JEROME
No trouble. We're ready.

INT. ARENA. MLS DANCE COUPLES FLAKED OUT
Camera moves from one tired couple to another. Some lying right on the dance floor. Some half asleep on chairs that rim the dance floor.

INT. ARENA PLATFORM MCU RED SKELTON
Red Skelton looks at his watch then, holding his microphone, he turns to Gerry Mann.

RED SKELTON
Hey Gerry…

INT ARENA PLATFORM MCU GERRY MANN AT PIANO
Gerry looks up from his piano

RED SKELTON (continuing Voice over)
Knock Knock.

> **GERRY MANN**
> Who's there?

> **RED**
> Time-fer

> **GERRY MANN**
> Time-fer who?

> **RED**
> Time-fer you to make music so
> these folks can dance.

Gerry gives an agreeing nod then gives a down beat As music begins Red picks up a large horn, gives a loud blast and announces

> **RED SKELTON**
> Come on dancers - Time to dance…

INT. ARENA - LS DANCERS GETTING BACK TO WORK.

INT. ARENA MCU RED SKELTON

> **RED SKELTON** (to audience)
> This is the start of hour seventy-two folks.
> Let's give 'em a big hand.

INT. ARENA AUDIENCE

Audience applauds as dancers try to look happy and rested. "Happy and rested" that is, if you think the fellow with number 18 on his back is "happy" almost carrying his sleeping partner. Or the girl who has number 6 resting his head on her shoulder.

Unforgettable Helen WGA 1867742					Phillips Wylly

INT. AUDITORIUM CU HELEN
    Helen's eyes are wide with amazement she has never seen anything like this. She is too overwhelmed to hear:

              RED SKELTON (off camera)
        Time for our new song bird Ladies and
        Gentlemen, Here's Helen double R Forrest.

INT ARENA PLATFORM CU HELEN
    She did not hear Red's intro.

INT. ARENA PLATFORM MCU JEROME (GERRY)
    In a loud stage whisper:

              JEROME (GERRY)
    (In the same voice we will remember from the stairway)
               Helen!

INT   PLATFORM MCU HELEN
    She hears Jerome for sure. Almost in a daze she gets to her feet and starts toward Red and the microphone. What is she to sing? Before her embarrassment can become public she realizes Gerry Mann and the orchestra are playing the wonderful song "Did You Ever See a Dream Walking," by Harry Revel and Mack Gordon.   One of her favorites. Mrs. S must have told him.

INT PLATFORM CU HELEN STEPS TO THE MICROPHONE AND BEGINS TO SING.

INT. ARENA VARIOUS SHOTS   (Helen's Voice over)
    Gerry Listening,   Red Skelton listening
    Dancers reacting to Helen's voice as they move about.
    A girl, looks up from partner's shoulder and waves. She loves what she is hearing.

INT. ARENA - HELEN (as she finishes song)
    Audience breaks into sincere applause. Even the dancers join in with hand waves and thumbs up signals.

Unforgettable Helen WGA 1867742   Phillips Wylly

ARENA PLATFORM
    Helen reacts to applause. She turns towards Red who gives her a big Thumbs Up. She turns to Gerry who signals her to come to him.

INT. ARENA PLATFORM MCU GERRY and HELEN

                  GERRY (while playing)
    That was really good..

                  HELEN
    Thank you. Thank you, Gerry..

                  GERRY
    Okay. Now if you're gonna be a regular,
    We'll have to find time to work out some
    arrangements.

ROTATE FRAME FROM ARENA STAGE TO

EXT. DAY LS BROOKLYN HIGH SCHOOL
    The tired old buildings look a bit intimidating - this is the architecture of the 1890's when this school was built.

INTERIOR DAY   VICE PRINCIPAL'S OFFICE.
    If the exterior looks intimidating that's nothing compared to the intimidation Helen feels as she stands before the Vice Principal. A pleasant looking woman but her pleasant looks make no impression on Helen. Being called to the Principal's Office - even the Vice principal's Office is a fate worse than death for students.

INT. VP OFFICE MCU HELEN AND VP

                  VICE PRINCIPAL
    Well Helen, I assume you would like to
    graduate with the rest of you class next
    June?

Unforgettable Helen WGA 1867742   Phillips Wylly

                    HELEN (Mumbles, intimidated)
                            Yes Mam.

                         VICE PRINCIPAL
               Then you better get down to work. The only subject
               you're doing well in is Music. Mr. Davis says
               you have an excellent voice and musical talent. But you
               need more than that to get ahead in today's world.
               You need an education and a diploma.

                              HELEN
               (nods again but this time the words come out)
                            Yes Mam.

                              VP
               Okay. You get busy then because if I don't
               see real improvement by next report card
               I will have to recommend you don't graduate.
               That means you repeat you senior year. Understand?

                              HELEN
               Yes mam, I understand. I'll study. I promise.

ROTATE FRAME MLS NIGHT CLUB STAGE
    Gerry Mann and the orchestra are playing. People are eating,
    drinking and dancing

INT. STAGE MCU HELEN seated behind a music stand. Obviously
    concentration on the score.

INT. STAGE MCU
    Over Helen's shoulder at music stand. Oh. Wait a minute, it isn't a
    music score she is concentrating on, it is.

INT. CU   GEOMETRY LESSON ON MUSIC STAND
     Helen's hand holding a pencil reaches in to note an answer.

Unforgettable Helen WGA 1867742   Phillips Wylly

INT. BANDSTAND MS HELEN BENT OVER GEOMETRY IN FOREGROUND, GERRY AT PIANO IN BG STARTS TUNE

                    GERRY (calling to Helen)
                    Helen...
(It is that same tone of voice we heard from the bottom of the stairs in the Silverman house.   A tone that gets Helen's immediate attention.)

INT   BANDSTAND MCU HELEN
Helen stands and starts toward mike

                    GERRY MANN (voice over)
          Time for our song bird again... here she is...

FAST FRAME ROTATION TO
EXT. DAY HIGH SCHOOL GRAD STAGE CU PRINCIPAL

                  WOMAN PRINCIPAL
                  Helen Fogel...

EXT DAY BROOKLYN HIGH SCHOOL ATHLETIC FIELD
The school does not look quite so intimidating today. Flags flying, crowds of people in the grandstand applauding. Graduation is underway. As Principle reads the name, student steps forward, VP hands them their diploma. Girl now stepping forward is Helen.

EXT. GRAD STAGE MCU as VP hands Helen her diploma

                  VICE PRINCIPAL
      Congratulations Helen. I knew you could do it.

                    HELEN
        Thank you. Thank you very much.

Unforgettable Helen WGA 1867742   Phillips Wylly

EXT   GRANDSTAND MS JEROME AND HONEY SILVERMAN
Cheers and tears of joy as Helen, clutching her diploma joins them

          HONEY SILVERMAN
Oh Helen. We are so proud of you.

          JEROME
Yes we are. Congratulations

          HELEN (As she gives each a hug.)
I owe it all to you. Thank you so much

          JEROME (Blinking back a tear)
Yes, well now maybe you will get yourself
over to Marshals and pick out some new music.
We got a job this summer you know.

EXT   DAY STREET   CU SIGN ABOVE STORE ENTRANCE
"MARSHALLS MUSIC"

INT   DAY - MARSHAL'S
The store is filled with music from a piano. Potential customers
select music scores. To decide if it is what they are seeking. they
take them to the pianist for him to play.

INT. MARSHAL'S. MS HELEN
Carefully sorting through sheet music Helen finally selects one:
"Deep Purple" by Peter De Rose

INT. STORE MS PIANIST & CUSTOMER AS HELEN APPROACHES
Smiling, waiting patiently Helen nods in time to the music. The
pianist finishes, hands music back to customer then turns to Helen.

          PIANIST
Hi Helen. What-cha got today?

Unforgettable Helen WGA 1867742   Phillips Wylly

                              HELEN
  (As she hands the music to pianist)
     This one really looks nice Mister Honthaner.

Mr. H takes the music, spreads it out on the piano music stand

                MR. HONTHANER (looking at music)
        Oh, hey. This is perfect for you.
 (He begins to play the Peter De Rose composition, "Deep Purple.")
             Come on, sing it Helen

CAMERA MOVES IN ON HELEN AS SHE SINGS

INT. STORE VARIOUS MCU SHOPPERS
    Shoppers stop what they are doing to listen as Helen sings

INT. STORE - CU MIDDLE AGE MAN LISTENING

INT. STORE. MR. H. LOOKS AT MIDDLE AGE MAN AND NODS

INT. STORE MCU MIDDLE AGE MAN NODS BACK

INT. STORE
    Helen finishes her song. There is applause from shoppers and the Middle Age Man.. Helen is slightly surprised, slightly embarrassed but she breaks into a smile and bows to the shoppers.

INT STORE MCU HELEN AND PIANIST

                          MR. H
    Helen, there's someone I want you to meet…

INT. STORE MS
    The Middle Age man joins Helen and the piano player…..

DISSOLVE

Unforgettable Helen WGA 1867742   Phillips Wylly

EXT. CONEY ISLAND BOARDWALK AND BEACH.   EVENING
It must be warm, there are almost as many people in bathing suits still on the beach as there are people dressed for evening heading to various   restaurants and lounges.

INT. NIGHT CLUB   NIGHT - CU MAN'S WATCH.
The time is almost seven o'clock

INT. CLUB. CAMERA PULLS BACK REVEALING GERRY MANN LOOKING UP FROM WATCH. CAMERA WIDENS AS MANN LOOKS OUT OVER NIGHT CLUB.

INT. CLUB LS ROOM
Over the heads of a good crowd of diners…There she is. At last.

INT. 4BAND STAND.
Helen hurries to take her place on the stand The band members nod and grin as an annoyed Gerry Mann welcomes her

> GERRY (looking at watch)
> You're late! Where you been?

> HELEN
> You wont believe.. Wait 'till I tell you

> GERRY (as band members listen)
> Tell me what?

> HELEN
> I got a day job. I'm gonna sing on
> (Now singing the once famous theme song)
> Double You En E Double You
> The station that is serving you
> New York and New Jersey too
> Twenty-four hours a day, that's true
> (Half the members of the orchestra join in singing the last line)
> That's W N E W!

Unforgettable Helen WGA 1867742   Phillips Wylly

>   GERRY
>   That's fine Helen, Now you ready to go to work here?

Helen nods "yes" Gerry gives a down beat and the music starts

INT NIGHT CLUB MCU HELEN STEPS TO MICROPHONE TO SING:
   Herb Brown, Arthur Freed song: You Were Meant For Me."

DISSOLVE

INT. SILVERMAN KITCHEN MID MORNING. CU RADIO
   It is Brunch time. Jerome/Gerry and wife Honey are munching toast
   and drinking coffee while listening to Helen's voice coming from
   radio speaker continuing song from last night

.INT SILVERMAN KITCHEN AS THEY LISTEN
   As song ends Jerome turns off radio and looks at his wife.

>   JEROME
>   So, what-a you think?
>
>   HONEY
>   I told you before, she's very good..
>
>   JEROME
>   Yes, she really is

Then, changing the subject, he picks up the copy of the musicians
magazine, DownBeat he had been reading.

>   JEROME/GERRY
>   Been reading about Artie…
>
>   HONEY
>   (As a bit of sadness comes over her face)
>   Ohhh…Jerr… Ever wish you had gone
>   with him when he started his group?

JEROME/GERRY
(He puts down the paper rather deliberately.)
No. Never Honey. This is what I want
You. Our home.. A chance to play with
my own group. A chance to help you teach.

Then turning back to the paper:

JEROME
But it says here Billie Holiday is leaving
Artie. That means he is going to need a new
Singer…

HONEY (reacting)
You think Helen?

JEROME
She would be perfect.

Jerome gets up from table and heads for the telephone hanging in the hall.

DISSOLVE:

INT. DAY LS GRAND CENTRAL STATION DAY
The giant clock tells us it is a few minutes after 7AM.
Music up: Duke Ellington and his Orchestra. 'Take The A Train'. "

INT. GRAND CENTRAL MS
Helen, Gerry/Jerome and Honey Silverman are trying to make their way through the crowd. It isn't easy, specially when you are not at all sure where you are going. Gerry is carrying a rather large, quite old suitcase and trying to find a sign to direct them to Track 15.

INT. STATION CU SIGN: TRACK 15 - ST. LOUIS EXPRESS

INT. STATION. MS HELEN AND THE SILVERMANS
Gerry sees the sign. Reacts with a sigh of relief, nods in that direction and heads that way.

INT. STATION LS TRACK 15 AND TRAIN
   The platform is crowded.. Somewhere in the mob Helen and the
   Silvermans are moving,.. Looking.., Helen's seat is in Car #4.

INT. TRACK 15 MCU (Music down under)
   Honey Silverman sees the car number, points

> HONEY
> Car number 4. There it is

INT. ENTRANCE TO CAR #4 MS
   Helen and the Silvermans climb the steps into the car

INT. CAR #4 MLS HELEN AND SILVERMANS
   As they make their way down the crowded aisle to seat #11.

> GERRY
> Here we are..

He lifts Helen's suitcase to the overhead rack

INT. RR CAR MCU
   It is time for good byes and this will not be easy. Helen, with tears in
   her eyes, looks to Gerry then throws her arms around Honey.

> HELEN
> Oh gosh. Do I really want to do this?

> HONEY
> Yes…you do. It's dream come true Helen.

> GERRY (trying to smile)
> Hell yes. This is the chance of a lifetime for you
> and a chance for us to get our guest room back.

Laughter and tears combine as Helen hugs Gerry

Unforgettable Helen WGA 1867742   Phillips Wylly

                              HELEN
              Thank you. Thank you, boss. I love you. I love you
              both so much. You're the mom and dad I didn't have.

INT. RR CAR MCU HELEN AND HONEY

                              HONEY (suddenly a bit serious)
              Be careful Helen. You'll be surrounded by
              a couple of dozen men who like pretty girls.

                              HELEN
              I know. I'll be careful. I'm gonna wait
              For the right one like you did.

INT. RR CAR ANOTHER ANGLE
    Another hug then Honey and Jerome break away and head up the
    aisle. As Helen watches them go Duke Ellington's "A Train" fades
    back in.

INT. RR CAR. MCU HELEN As she sits in her seat then looks out the
    window at

INT. / EXT. RR PLATFORM MS FROM HELEN'S POV (POINT OF VIEW)
    Honey and Gerry standing on the platform below as the train
    slowly starts to move. Honey and Jerome with obvious affection for
    each other wave to Helen and the departing train.

EXT. MCU HONEY AND GERRY/JEROME ON PLATFORM
    As they watch the train leaving.

                              HONEY (Tearfully)
              She's the daughter we never had.

    And "A Train" fills the sound track.

Unforgettable Helen WGA 1867742　　　　　　　　　　　Phillips Wylly

INT. RR CAR. CU HELEN
   Tears in her eyes. She takes a deep breath then whispers to herself

                        HELEN
   They love each other so…. Maybe someday…

(Ellington "A Train" music back up.)

SLOW DISSOLVE

EXT. DAY SEVERAL SHOTS TRAIN UNDERWAY
HELEN IN WINDOW LOOKING OUT. (music continues)

DISSOLVE

INTERIOR. DAY ST. LOUIS RR STATION. (Music under and out)
   Series of shots as Helen lugging her suitcase, emerges from RR Car, makes her way to "Information" desk.

INT. RR STATION MS INFORMATION DESK
   Music out as Helen walks to the desk and asks the attendant

                        HELEN
   How do I get to the Sattler Hotel please.

                        ATTENDANT
   (Obviously an over worked, unhappy with his job fellow)
   Bus Number Seven

Before Helen can ask anything more he turns away to deal with the another questioner. Helen looks about. The suitcase is getting heavier all the time. Where is the bus? Oh. There…

INT. CU BUS #7 SIGN

INT. STATION SEVERAL SHOTS
   Helen makes her way to the bus. The suitcase is getting heaver and heaver as she climbs stair into the bus.

Unforgettable Helen WGA 1867742   Phillips Wylly

INT. BUS
Helen puts the suitcase down as she talks to the bus driver

                 HELEN
         How long to the Stattler Hotel

INT. BUS - MCU DRIVER
               BUS DRIVER
         About fifteen minutes mam.

                 HELEN
         Will you let me know when we get there please

               BUS DRIVER
         Yes,- mam, you bet.

INT. BUS. MS
Helen thanks driver, lifts suitcase and starts down the aisle. She spots an empty space in the overhead rack with an empty seat beneath it. She does not see the white line painted across the aisle

INT. BUS MS
Helen reaches the rack and empty seat. Before she can start to lift the case a black hand reaches for it and a man's voice tells her

               BLACK MAN
         Let me get that fo you mam.

                 HELEN
         Oh, thank you. I'm not sure I could have
         made it.

INT. BUS HELEN AND BLACK MAN
The black man easily lifts the case and places it on the rack. As he does Helen sinks into the empty seat. She's hardly down before

               BLACK MAN
         Don't sit <u>there</u> mam

Unforgettable Helen WGA 1867742   Phillips Wylly

INT. BUS MS DRIVER (looking back at Helen)

>BUS DRIVER
>Don't sit there Miss. Come up ahead of the line.

INT. BUS MS HELEN AND BLACK MAN

>HELEN to Black Man
>Line? What line?

>BLACK MAN pointing
>That white line up there mam.

INT. BUS CU WHITE LINE PAINTED ACROSS AISLE

INT. BUS HELEN AND BLACK MAN

>BLACK MAN
>You white folk sit up FRONT.
>Us black folk sit back here.

Stunned, Helen does not know what to do.

>BLACK MAN
>Don't worry none 'bout yo suitcase. I keep a eye on it.
>You go-head up dere.

>HELEN (somewhat confused)
>Alright. Thank you

.INT BUS MS BUS DRIVER

>BUS DRIVER
>There's a seat right up here Miss.

Helen goes to the seat the driver is indicating. She sits and the bus gets underway.

Unforgettable Helen WGA 1867742 　　　　　　　　　　　Phillips Wylly

EXT. DAY ST. LOUIS STREETS
    Bus #7 makes its way through down town St. Louis traffic .

INT. BUS. MS DRIVER AND STREET
    As bus stops in front of Hotel driver calls to Helen

>BUS DRIVER
>Here we are Miss.

INT. BUS. MS
    Helen gets to her feet and starts to go back down the aisle to get her suitcase but the black man has already lifted the case down and is headed up the aisle towards Helen.

>BLACK MAN
>I got it mam.

EXT. BUS. A BEAUTIFUL AFTERNOON
    Helen comes down the bus steps followed by her Black friend. He sets the case down and signals to

EXT HOTEL MS HOTEL DOOR MAN
    Who comes to get Helen's case

EXT HOTEL BUS STOP - HELEN AND BLACK FRIEND

>HELEN (to black friend)
>Thank you. Thank you so much. I don't really understand all this but you have been very kind.

>BLACK MAN
>You welcome, mam. Enjoy yo stay.

He climbs back into the bus and gives her a wave as the bus door closes and the bus pulls away.

Unforgettable Helen WGA 1867742   Phillips Wylly

EXT. DAY HOTEL ENTRANCE
    The doorman picks up Helen's suitcase and directs her towards the impressive entrance to this fine old hotel.

INT. HOTEL MLS
    Helen walks to the front desk.

.INT. HOTEL FRONT DESK MS

              DESK CLERK
           Good afternoon Miss.

                  HELEN
       A reservation for Helen Forrest?

          DESK CLERK (with some enthusiasm)
    Yes indeed Miss Forrest. Welcome to St. Louis.

(He passes her a registration form to sing)

              DESK CLERK
      I know Mister Shaw is expecting you.
      I'll let him know you're here.

INT. HOTEL DESK
    As Helen registers Clerk signals for a bell boy

           DESK CLERK (to bell boy)
             Room 1403.

(He hands key to bell boy.)

INT. HOTEL LOBBY LS
    Bell boy takes Helen's case and leads her to the elevators.

Unforgettable Helen WGA 1867742   Phillips Wylly

INT. ELEVATOR MS HELEN AND BELL BOY ENTER

           BELLBOY (to elevator operator)
    Fourteen, please.

(Then, as door closes he turns back to Helen)

    You're going to sing with Artie Shaw aren't you?

           HELEN
    If he likes my voice…

           BELL BOY
    Oh I know he will.

           HELEN
    I hope so.

INT. ELEVATOR DOOR OPENS INTO HALL
Helen and bell boy exit elevator. Bell Boy leads the way hall to Room 1403, He opens it then steps aside to let Helen enter.

INT. HOTEL ROOM. DAY
The late afternoon sun is shining through the window as Bell Boy places Helen's case on the luggage stand. He hands the key to Helen

           BELL BOY (pointing)
    There's the bathroom.
  (He points again)
      …The closet. Anything you need Miss Forrest,
    Just pick up the phone and let us know.

Bell Boy stalling, waiting for a tip

           BELL BOY
    Oh, I didn't check the towels…

Unforgettable Helen WGA 1867742   Phillips Wylly

INT. HOTEL ROOM MS BELLBOY OPENS BATHROOM DOOR,
LOOKS IN. THEN TURNS BACK TO HELEN.

                      BELL BOY
They look fine…If there is anything else…
Just pick up the phone and ask for
Room Service….

INT. ROOM MCU HELEN.
Her hotel experience has been very limited but she slowly gets the message. She opens her hand bag, finds two quarters and hands then to Bell boy
                      HELEN
Thank you. Thank you very much

                      BELL BOY
(Taking the quarters In those days fifty cents was a good tip.) .
Oh thank you Miss Forrest. And good luck
with Artie Shaw. I know he's gonna like you.

INT. HOTEL ROOM
As the Bell Boy leaves the camera centers on Helen. She takes a deep breath and looks around. It is all a bit overwhelming. She walks to the easy chair and plops into the seat. Another deep breath. She looks at the phone. She must call Mrs. Silverman and Gerry to tell them she has arrived. But before she can do this,

INT. TELEPHONE CU
The phone starts to ring. Camera widens to show Helen as she picks up the phone.
                      HELEN (in to phone)
Hello… (Then a bit stunned) Oh, Mr Shaw…
                  (Pause as she listens)
Alright, Artie. And yes, it was a wonderful trip.
                  (She listens some more)
Oh sure I feel great. Excited but great.
                  (She listens…)
The Sky Terrace? Okay, be right there.

INT. HOTEL ROOM CU HELEN ON PHONE

                    HELEN
She is about to hang up, then…
          Oh. Wait. Where is The Sky Terrace?

(She listens again)
          That shouldn't be too hard to find.
          I'm on the way.

INT. ROOM
Helen jumps out of the chair and heads out the door.

INT. LOBBY AREA OUTSIDE SKY TERRACE
A man is waiting for the elevator door to open.
A moment later it does and Helen steps out. Man goes to her.

                  JIM WOOLLEY
Hi Helen, I'm Jim Woolley. That's W<u>OO</u>LL<u>E</u>Y. Two O's and two Ls. Beats two R's, right?

                  HELEN
(A bit confused but laughing none the less.)
          Yes, I guess so.

                  JIM WOOLLEY
I'm Artie's Band Manager. Thought I should catch you out here. You could spend all afternoon trying to find a door that isn't locked

                  HELEN
Hello double L double O. Nice to meet you.
(She extends her hand for a hand shake.)

                  JIM WOOLLEY
(As he shakes her hand)
          I know the boss told you to call him Artie
          So you better call me Jim.

                    HELEN (laughing))
                Okay. Hello Jim.

INT. LOBBY AREA
    Jim takes Helen's arm and steers her to one of the several doorways

                    JIM
                Come on. Artie and Jerry are waitin' for you.

                    HELEN (as they head for door)
                I know who Artie is, but who's Jerry?
                I know it isn't Gerry Mann.

                    JIM (with a chuckle)
                No. This one is Jerry Gray. He's our arranger.

    They reach the door. Jim opens it for Helen and she looks in

INT. LS SKY TERRACE BALLROOM - HELEN'S POV
    Lovely room with rows of tables, then a dance floor, then a
    bandstand. And above it all, a glass ceiling open to the sky.

INT. MCU HELEN AND JIM AT BALLROOM DOORWAY.
    This ballroom is the grandest she has ever seen. She looks to Jim

                    HELEN
                Nothing like this in Coney Island.

                    JIM
                Maybe not. It's pretty nice isn't it.

INT. BALLROOM MS BAND STAND
    Two men are on the band stand. Artie Shaw standing. Jerry Gray
    seated at piano. As they see Helen and Jim, Jerry stands, Artie
    steps down off stand and heads toward them

Unforgettable Helen WGA 1867742   Phillips Wylly

INT. BALLROOM ENTRANCE AREA. NEW ANGLE AS ARTIE ARRIVES TO WELCOME HELEN

> ARTIE SHAW
> Hi Helen. You're even prettier than Gerry said.

> HELEN
> Wow! I sure hope you like my voice
> 'cause I certainly want to work for you!

> ARTIE
> I don't think that will be a problem.

(He takes her arm and leads her towards the band stand)

> ARTIE (continuing)
> Come on. Jerry's been working on a couple
> of arrangements for you.

INT. BALLROOM. CAMERA FOLLOWS HELEN, ARTIE AND JIM AS THEY WALK TO BANDSTAND.

There is a chair on the first level just in front of the piano. Artie points to it.

> ARTIE
> That's where you'll sit young lady.

INT. MCU ARTIE AND HELEN as he is pointing.

> HELEN (excited, almost overwhelmed)
> Oh…Gee

Then, after looking again toward the orchestra set up

> HELEN
> Where does Billy Holiday sit. I can't wait
> To meet her. She's so great.

ARTIE
You'll meet her tonight but she
doesn't sit on the bandstand

HELEN (puzzled)
She doesn't? How come?...

ARTIE
It's the damn black and white thing.
Black can't sit with white.

HELEN (in wonderment and disgust)
Like the line in the bus...

INT. BANDSTAND
As Artie, Helen and Jim reach where Jerry is waiting. He sticks out his hand to shake Helen's

JERRY GRAY
Hi Helen. Been hearin' great things about you.

HELEN (Taking his hand)
Hello... Hope I can live up to 'em.

JERRY (with a grin)
Well let's check it out....

(He sits at the piano.)

JERRY GRAY
Word is you kind-a like "All The Things You Are".
Let's try it.

INT. BANDSTAND MS HELEN AND JERRY
(NOTE: We may want a bit of musician talk here. About tempo, octave. Then)
As Jerry starts to play, Helen turns to Artie'

INT. BALLROOM STAGE - MCU HELEN AND ARTIE

                HELEN
If Billy Holiday can't sit on the stand then
I don't want to either.

Before Artie can respond, Helen turns back to Jerry Gray and begins to sing the Jerome Kern/Oscar Hammerstein hit
" ALL THE THINGS YOU ARE."

DISSOLVE (Helen's song continues)

INT. NIGHT. LS HELEN ON STAGE. BALLROOM FILLED WITH PEOPLE.
Helen, now standing at microphone in front of full orchestra Continues singing "All The Things You Are" People are dancing, listening, enjoying their evening out.

INT. NIGHT LS BALLROOM   Applause as Helen finishes.
Helen smiles, curtseys, then heads off stage.

INT. REAR OF BALLROOM. MCU
JIM WOOLLEY and another man standing just inside the entrance doors applauding
                OTHER MAN
You wanna know something, She's great.

Man takes Jim's arm and sort of pulls him out the door as Artie and the band strike up "Indian Love Call"

                MAN (continuing)
Now let's get some work done. Shall we?

INT. BALLROOM ANGLE ON ARTIE AND YOUNG DANCERS
Several dancers shouting, "Begin The Beguine" and others try to reach out to Artie. Wanting autographs or just to touch the great man.

INT. LOBBY OUTSIDE THE BALLROOM. (Shaw music in BG)
Man and Jim walk to a door off the lobby. Door leads to a small office. They enter.

.INT. OFFICE.
Man points to a chair in front of desk.

      MAN
Grab a chair. I got a check for you
And a contract for two weeks in December.

      JIM (as he takes check and signs contract)
Okay, Okay,, Come on. Billy goes on in
a second and I don't want to miss her last stand.

INT. BALLROOM - LS THEN ZOOM IN TO CU BILLIE HOLIDAY AS SHE WALKS TO MICROPHONE TO SING JIMMIE RODGERS: "ANY OLD TIME."

INT. BALLROOM OFF STAGE. MCU HELEN WATCHING AND LISTENING. There is no doubt about how Helen feels about Billie's singing

INT. STAGE CU BILLIE FINISHING SONG

INT. REAR OF BALLROOM. MCU JIM WOOLLEY
Applauding vigorously.

      JIM (more or less to himself.)
So good. My god we're gome miss you.

INT. LS BALLROOM STAGE AND AUDIENCE
Some applause as Billie leaves microphone and walks off stage. As she does there are more calls for "Begin the Beguine," and Artie starts playing it.

INT. BACK STAGE MS
    Helen waits as Billie Holiday walks towards her. Camera moves in as the two get closer.   Helen throws her arms around Billie.

              HELEN
    Oh Billie. I wish you weren't going.
    I love to listen to you sing. You're so great.

              BILLIE
    You ain't too bad yourself young lady.

              HELEN (disregarding Billie's compliment)
    Why can't you stay?

              BILLIE
    'Cause I can't take it anymore Helen. I can't…
    Can't stay in the same hotel you stay in.
    Can't eat in the same restaurant. Can't use the same bathroom. Can't drink from the same fountain.
    Can't even sit on the stage.

              HELEN (to Billie)
    Oh Billie. This is so wrong.

INT. STAGE   MLS MUSIC ENDS AND ARTIE STARTS OFF STAGE.
    Young jitter bugs screaming "Artie! Artie!"

INT. BACKSTAGE. MS ARTIE APPROACHING
    (Muttering as he walks toward Billie and Helen.)

              ARTIE SHAW
    Jesus, how much longer can I take those kids!

(As he reaches Billie and Helen - to Billie)
              ARTIE
    One of these days I'm gonna leave too.
(Artie puts his arm around Billie.)
    I'm gonna miss you. We all are.

Unforgettable Helen WGA 1867742   Phillips Wylly

INT   MCU BILLIE
>   BILLIE
> I'll miss you too boss. We gave it a good try.

MCU ARTIE AND BILLIE
>   ARTIE
> I think we did.   Maybe it will help.

CU - HELEN WITH TEARS IN HER EYES AS SHE LOOKS ON.

MLS BACKSTAGE
Many of the musicians have gathered around Helen, Artie and Billie all wanting to tell her goodbye as JIM WOOLLEY walks in

>   JIM WOOLLEY (Clapping his hands)
> Okay everybody. Bus is waiting. Come on.
> Let's get with it.

INT. BACK STAGE - MS WOOLLEY AND BILLIE
Camera moves in on Jim as he walks to Billie. picks up her bag, puts an arm around her and leads her

>   JIM WOOLLEY
> Billie, Come on. Got a cab waiting for you.

INT./EXT. BACKSTAGE MLS
Billie hugs WOOLLEY then, with tears in her eyes, goes with him out the door.

INT. BACK STAGE CU HELEN WATCHES HER LEAVE

EXT. NIGHT. LS BUS AT STAGE DOOR.
Musicians are climbing on board. Some carrying instruments, luggage, etc.

EXT. NIGHT MS STAGE DOOR AS HELEN EMERGES
Helen is carrying the gown she wore on stage. She sees Jim at the bus door.

                    HELEN (to Jim)
They took my suitcase. What-a I do with this dress?
(She holds up the dress.)

EXT. MCU WOOLLEY
                    WOOLLEY
Hang it on the rack at the back of the bus

INT. BUS
Helen climbs up steps, walks down the aisle to rear of bus.

INT. BUS. MCU CLOTHING RACK
Helen hangs dress and sits down with a bit of a sigh. It has been a long day.

INT. BUS MCU HELEN SEATED
She has no more than relaxed when a voice calls to her.

                    OFF CAMERA VOICE
Helen. Don't sit back there.

INT. FRONT OF BUS - MCU JIM WOOLLEY
(the off camera voice) standing just inside the bus looking back at Helen.

                    WOOLLEY (continuing)
Come on up front.

INT. BUS MCU HELEN

                    HELEN (Looking at Jim)
There can't be a white lines in here.

INT. BUS MCU WOOLLEY

                    WOOLLEY (with a chuckle)
No… No it's more of a blue line.
When those guys start smoking their shit
you won't be able to breath. Come up here
and sit by an open window.

INT. BUS MCU HELEN
She rolls her eyes with a "Jesus what next?" expression, gets to her feet and walks up the aisle to the front row seat Jim has saved for her.

EXT. NIGHT. LS BUS AS IT PULLS OUT.

INT. BUS. MS
Helen seated next to window. Well behind her there is a haze of blue smoke beginning to form She sniffs. Turns and looks back.

INT. BUS. MS MUSICIANS SEATED IN REAR.
Several are already smoking. Others are getting ready.

INT. BUS. CU HELEN
OMG! She turns to the window, opens it and sticks her head half way out. Thank god for some fresh air.

EXT NIGHT SEVERAL SHOTS OF BUS AS IT MAKES ITS WAY DOWN THE HIGHWAY AND NIGHT BECOMES DAY
Music under travel shots = Artie Shaw "Lambeth Walk".

EXT. DAY MCU "STATE THEATRE" MARQUEE (Music under)

              "ARTIE SHAW ORCHESTRA"

Camera pans away to band bus as it passes and rounds corner.

EXT - "STAGE DOOR" SIGN OVER DOORWAY AS BUS PULLS UP.

Unforgettable Helen WGA 1867742   Phillips Wylly

EXT. DAY. MS JIM WOOLLEY AT BUS DOOR
    Music out as door opens and musicians start getting off

                   JIM WOOLLEY
        OK everybody. We're on in less than an hour.

EXT. BUS DOOR MCU JIM AND HELEN
    Jim offers a hand to Helen as she steps down carrying her dress,

                 WOOLLEY (chuckling)
        So how did you like your first bus ride?

                    HELEN
        Don't ask. I didn't sleep a wink and the
        smell on my dress is probably gonna give me
        a high all day long.

    With that Helen walks away following musicians to Stage Door.

INT. MLS STAGE. REAR VIEW OF MOVIE SCREEN SHOWING NEWSREEL TITLE (backwards) CAMERA PANS TO BAND STAND WHERE MUSICIANS ARE GETTING SEATED.

INT. STAGE. MCU HELEN FINDING HER SEAT.
    She watches activity This is all amazing

INT. STAGE
    Several shots as Curtain closes over Newsreel End Title. The screen elevates into the rafter above the stage. As the curtain opens Artie gives a downbeat, Theme music begins and Spot lights find Artie.

    From the theme music to an upbeat "curtain riser" is an easy transition for Artie and the band. For a wide eyed Helen Forrest it is all unbelievable. Kids in audience crowding down to the band stand. Reaching out to grab Artie. Tony Pastor as he stands to play his alto sax solo. As music ends:

Unforgettable Helen WGA 1867742   Phillips Wylly

INT. STAGE MCU ARTIE SHAW AT MIKE

> ARTIE
> Now a special treat. Our new vocalist
> Miss Helen Forrest.

INT - STAGE FROM AUDIENCE POV.
Camera zooms in on Helen as she walks to microphone and sings The Mergan Lewis/Nancy Hamilton hit song, "HOW HIGH THE MOON."

INT. LS THEATRE AS HELEN LEAVES STAGE KIDS APPLAUD AND SHOUTS OF "BEGIN THE BEGUINE" CAN BE HEARD AS KIDS REACH OUT TO GRAB AT ARTIE.

DISOLVE

EXT - NIGHT. MLS STAGE DOOR AND BUS -
Musicians leaving and getting on bus.

EXT. NIGHT MCU HELEN CARRYING HER DRESS
As Helen heads for the bus a voice calls to her

> OFF CAMERA VOICE
> Hey Helen…

Helen stops and looks toward off screen voice

EXT. NIGHT MCU ARTIE SHAW

> ARTIE (the off camera voice)
> Jim says bus travel doesn't work to good for you.
> Wanna ride with us?

EXT NIGHT CU HELEN
> HELEN
> Oh Wow! Yes!

EXT NIGHT MS ARTIE'S CAR
   Jim holds front passenger open for her as Helen joins him and Artie

EXT. NIGHT. LS HIGH ANGLE ARTIE'S CAR PULLS AWAY
   (Music: Shaw Theme "Nightmare" softly in background)

INT. CAR. NIGHT (Music continues)
   Helen and Jim (in back seat) sit quietly while Artie carefully winds his way through city streets. Now as they reach open road, without taking his eyes off the road, Music under as Artie breaks silence.

> ARTIE (to Helen)
> So, how's it going for you so far?

> HELEN
> Oh Artie, I'm just so thrilled to be here
> singing for you. It's a dream come true.

> ARTIE
> Good. That's good. I hope it can stay
> that way for you for a long time.

INT CAR - NIGHT CU HELEN
   A moment of thought. What exactly is he saying?... Then

> HELEN
> Isn't it that way for you? Making music I mean.
> Having people love what you are doing?

INT CAR. CU ARTIE

> ARTIE
> Making music, yes. But people loving it...
> Not so much. I'm sick and tired of listening to
> them screaming "Beguine," or "Love Call."
> or anything else we play over and over again.
> I got-a move on, got-a do new things.
> If somebody told Beethoven to stick with his
> Eighth Symphony he'd never have written his ninth.

Unforgettable Helen WGA 1867742   Phillips Wylly

INT. CAR. NIGHT. POV HIGHWAY AHEAD

INT. CAR NIGHT BACK TO HELEN ARTIE AND JIM

> JIM (from back seat)
> Helen, You and Billie seemed to hit it off pretty good.

> HELEN
> Oh she's so wonderful. I wish things could be better for her

> HELEN (After thoughtful pause)
> How can people be so cruel? The things they put her
> through. The names they call her.
> I remember kids in school used to call me, "A Jew"
> like Jew was a dirty word. And "Kike." but that was
> nothing compared to what they call her…

EXT. EARLY MORNING LS ARTIE'S CAR AS IT TRAVELS DOWN THE HIGHWAY LINED WITH BLOOMING FLOWERS

DISOLVE

EXT DAY FIELD COVERED WITH SNOW

DISSOLVE:

EXT NIGHT LIT THEATER MARQUE: "ARTIE SHAW. HELEN FORREST"

INT   MLS SHAW BAND ON STAND. HELEN AT MIKE SINGING: "MOONRAY"   A song written by Artie with Paul Madison and Arthur Quinzer.

ROTATE FRAME

EXT   SHAW BAND ON STAND (another location)   HELEN AT MIKE
   Singing the Lew Brown/Charles Tobias hit:
      COMES LOVE NOTHIN' CAN BE DONE

Unforgettable Helen WGA 1867742   Phillips Wylly

DISSOLVE:

INT. CU SIGN: "MERRY CHRISTMAS. CELEBRATE THE SEASON WITH ARTIE SHAW, HELEN FORREST. IN THE GOLD DUST ROOM."

INT LS GOLD DUST ROOM. STAGE HELEN AT MIKE SINGING: "JIMMY VAN HEUSEN'S HIT :

"DEEP IN A DREAM"

INT. STAGE APPLAUSE AS HELEN FINISHES SONG THEN LOUD SHOUTS OF "BEGIN THE BEGUINE.

INT STAGE. MCU ARTIE AS HE GIVES DOWN BEAT FOR "BEGUINE"   THEN WALKS OFF THE STAGE.

    ARTIE (to Tony Pastor as he passes)
   Take over Tony. I'm through!

INT. BACKSTAGE.   ARTIE WALKING INTO BACKSTAGE AREA.
 Jim Woolley hurries up to him. (Music in background)
    JIM
  What's up? You okay?

    ARTIE
  No, I'm not okay. I'm through.
  Tony's got the band. Bring everybody up
  to my room when they come off.

Then, almost ignoring Jim Woolley, Artie walks off.

INT ARTIE'S HOTEL ROOM CU OPEN SUITCASE
 Tha half packed suitcases lies on the bed. Camera pulls back to reveal Artie putting clothing into bag as Helen and band members enter.

Unforgettable Helen WGA 1867742 Phillips Wylly

                 ARTIE (turning to group)
Okay everybody. Thanks for coming up here. I want you to know this is it for me. Tony, you take the band. I'm finished. I'm gonna miss all you guys but I've had it with the kids. Now everybody out, while I finish packing.

INT. MCU ARTIE AS HE SHAKES A HAND, PATS A BACK, SAYS GOODBYE. THEN TURNS BACK TO SUITCASES ON THE BED.

                 HELEN (off screen voice)
                 Can I help you pack?

                 ARTIE
(Trying not to show surprise turns to look at Helen)
        Yeah, there's some shirts in that drawer.

Then, half laughing,
                 ARTIE
          Okay. What's on your mind?

INT   HOTEL ROOM   MCU HELEN AND ARTIE

                 HELEN
The first day I met you, almost two
years ago, you told me to call you Artie.
Now I'd like to call you Mr. Shaw...

                 ARTIE
(with a head nod and a bit of a smile.)
                 Okay

                 HELEN
Mr. Shaw, I want to thank you. I want to
thank you for giving me... I don't even know
what to call it...A chance to sing for you.
To be part of the most wonderful music
organization in the world.

(tears are now streaming from Helen's eyes)

Artie steps to Helen, puts a hand on her shoulder.

                  ARTIE
Yeah, we've been pretty successful. And a lot of our success has been because of you, Helen. So thank <u>you</u>. I'm finished but your just beginning. Now clear out-a here an' let me pack.

INT. ROOM MS AS HELEN STARTS FOR DOOR

                  ARTIE
Oh, by the way, word is Louise Tobin's leaving Benny. I hear he's a cheap son-of-a-bitch and friendly as a clam but he sure knows how to make music.

Unforgettable Helen WGA 1867742   Phillips Wylly

INT. DAY. BENNY GOODMAN SEATED IN FRONT OF MUSIC STAND PLAYING SOMETHING CLASSICAL ON THE CLARINET.
As Benny plays we become aware of the winter weather seen through the nearby window. After a moment or two a ringing telephone can be heard. At first Benny ignores it then, with a look of some annoyance, he picks up the phone;

                BENNY
        Yeah, what'cha want?
(a pause as he listens)
        Oh, Okay. Put her on.
(another pause)
        Hi Pops. I heard Artie quit. What's up?
(he listens)
        Yeah. Her baby is due pretty soon.
        You lookin' for a job?
(He listens)
        Okay. You got it. Eighty-five a week.

Benny listens for a moment then, almost laughing,

                BENNY
        One seventy-five! No wonder he quit.
        He went broke. It's eight-five here.
        Take it or leave it Pops.
            (pause as he listens)
        Okay. When can you be here?

INT/EXT   NIGHT - LOVERS LANE - CU CAR RADIO
Hand reaches for radio and turns it on. Music up as radio voice announces
                RADIO VOICE
        From Chicago's Crystal Ballroom it's the music of
        Benny Goodman and his Orchestra
Camera now pulls back and we are looking from the back seat of a car. Young couple in front seat are smooching as they listen Camera tilts up to reveal Chicago's Night lit skyline across the lake

Unforgettable Helen WGA 1867742   Phillips Wylly

                    HELEN'S VOICE
            From Car Radio - Singing Elsie Carlisle's hit:
                    SHAKE DOWN THE STARS

DISSOLVE

INT. NIGHT. CHICAGO BALLROOM HELEN AT MIKE
SONG CONTINUES AS CAMERA PULLS BACK FROM
HELEN AND GOODMAN BAND ON STAGE.

INT.   CU MOTION PICTURE CAMERA LENS
       Frame slowly widens and we find we are on a small motion
       picture stage. There is a lot of activity as orchestra desks
       are being set up, film director is positioning camera, etc.

INT   MOTION PICTURE STAGE.
       MS Helen and Ziggy Elmann (trumpet player) making their
            way to stage positions.

                        ZIGGY
                You made some of these with
                Artie I guess?

                        HELEN
                Yes. We made four or five. I
                Remember Artie called them "soundies."

INT. STAGE. MS
       Benny Goodman arrives. As he passes Helen and Ziggy
                        HELEN
                Good morning' boss

Goodman continues on with barely a nod of his head

55

Unforgettable Helen WGA 1867742   Phillips Wylly

INT. STAGE   MCU HELEN AND ZIGGY

           HELEN
    (shaking her head and half laughing)

Well he did nod... I think.

INT STAGE. MCU FILM DIRECTOR, CAMERA AND CAMERAMAN.

           DIRECTOR (to cameraman)
           OK, you all set?

           CAMERAMAN
           Yeah. Ready to roll.

Director turns to look towards

INT. STAGE   MS   BENNY AND BAND

           DIRECTOR (Voice Over)
    Okay Benny?

           BENNY
    Ready, pops.

INT STAGE MCU DIRECTOR & CAMERAMAN

           DIRECTOR
           Okay, Roll 'em.

           CAMERAMAN
    Speed.

Unforgettable Helen WGA 1867742   Phillips Wylly

>   DIRECTOR
>   And Action!

INT. STAGE MCU BENNY AS HE GIVES DOWNBEAT
>   Pull back to full screen band as they begin
>   "MOTHER MAY I GO OUT DANCING?"

INT. STAGE. MS HELEN JOINS BENNY AND THEY SING
>   Jack Lawrence's delightful song.

INT STAGE   CAMERA RUNNING (Song continues)

INT. MOVIE THEATRE PROJECTION BOOTH   CU
REEL OF FILM TURNING AS PROJECTOR RUNS
>   Music continues as projector runs and we   Pan
>   to follow projection beam to the far away screen
>   where we see the Black @ White "soundie"

>   HELEN & BENNY DUET
>   Yes, my darling daughter

INT. DAY MCU ELEVATOR DOORS.
>   Doors open into a business building hallway. Early morning sun
>   streaming in through a nearby window almost blinds Helen as she
>   steps out of elevator.

INT. HALLWAY.
>   MS Helen as she looks left and right then seeing her destination.

INT HALLWAY CU SIGN ON DOOR "COLUMBIA RECORDS ."

INT HALLWAY MS AS HELEN OPENS DOOR AND ENTERS.

Unforgettable Helen WGA 1867742   Phillips Wylly

INT. STUDIO ENTRANCE LOBBY. MS
    There is no one in the lobby. Helen is a bit surprised. She looks around. There is an open door leading to the control room. Helen walks to open door and sticks her head in.

                        HELEN
            Hello? Anybody here?

INT. CONTROL ROOM MS
    A young man looks out from behind a panel of some sort. Sees Helen

                    YOUNG MAN
       Hi Miss Forrest. What are you doing here this early?

INT. CONTROL ROOM MCU HELEN

                    HELEN (Reacting)
        Early? It's practically eight o'clock.

INT CONTROL ROOM   MCU YOUNG MAN

                    YOUNG MAN
      Yeah, that's right but you guys aren't
      due until nine.

INT. CONTROL ROOM   MCU HELEN

                  HELEN (as she reacts.)
      Son of a gun. That damn Ziggy Elman
      told me eight o'clock..

                    YOUNG MAN
    Well, I got a pot of fresh coffee and the paper
    if you wanna read it. My name's Pete, by the way."

                    HELEN
        Thanks Pete, you're a gentleman which
        is more than I can say for those clowns in the band.
        Coffee would be great, but I'll skip the paper
        if you'll let me watch what you're doing and tell me
        how all that stuff works.

INT. CONTROL ROOM CU PETE

                    PETE (with a chuckle)
        Sounds good to me, Nothing I like better
        than showing off for a beautiful women..

INT. CONTROL ROOM MCU HELEN & PETE

                    HELEN
        Flattery wont get you very far but the coffee might.

Pete ducks behind a large control panel. A moment later he reappears
with a cup of coffee in his hand which he gives to Helen.

                    PETE
        Careful It's hot.

As Helen takes a tentative sip, Pete opens a cabinet and takes out a
large black disk that looks like an oversize phonograph record.

INT. CONTROL ROOM VARIOUS SHOTS AS PETE EXPLAINS

                    PETE
        Okay, this is a blank recording disk.
    (He shows it to Helen.)
            You can see it has grooves in it, just like the
            Records you buy in the store, but it ain't got no
            music in it yet.

                    HELEN (as she looks on)
        Okay, How do it get music in it Mister Bones?

                  PETE
Ah, that's where it gets technical. Music, all sound
not just music, all sound is nothing but vibrations.
Vibrations that the hairs in your ears turn into sound.

                  HELEN
I think you just said I have hairy ears, but go ahead.

                  PETE (as he points and demonstrates.)
This turntable is just about like the one you
have at home, the big difference is the stylus.

                  HELEN
What do you mean. I've got plenty of style.

                  PETE
Okay. Will it make you happier if I call it
a phonograph needle? Even a singer must know
what a phonograph needle is.

                  HELEN
You just lost a dozen flattery points, but go ahead.

                  PETE
Okay. The band plays, you sing the microphones
 transmits those vibrations through the control panel
and then to this needle.

INT   CONTROL ROOM CU NEEDLE

                  PETE ((voice over)
Only this needle isn't a playback needle,
    it's a cutting stylus. As it vibrates it cuts
    little... I guess you could call them
    "notches" in the disk.

INT CONTROL ROOM MS HELEN AND PETE

                  HELEN
        Is that why I see you guys brushing
        little strings of thread away from the record?

                  PETE
        Yes. The stylus… the needle, is cutting
        Into the disc and as it cuts it causes those
        fine little threads. They're what you might
        think of a saw dust. I carefully brush
t   them away so they don't interfere with the
        needle's vibrations. So, the band plays,
        you sing, the <u>stylus</u> cuts the vibrations into
        the disk and we have a recording.

INT   CONTROL ROOM CU HELEN
Helen blinks a couple of times and takes a sip of her now cold coffee.

                  HELEN
        Pete, I think I understood most
        everything you said. Thank you.

INT. CONTROL ROOM ENTRANCE
The door swings open and Ziggy Elman looks in

                  ZIGGY
        Helen. You're on time for a change.

INT. CONTROL ROOM MCU HELEN AND ZIGGY

                  HELEN
        Very funny Zig. I'll get you later.

                  ZIGGY
Yeah, well that's sort-a what I had in mind. We got several
hours off after this…I was hoping I could take you somewhere
For a drink and something to eat.

Unforgettable Helen WGA 1867742   Phillips Wylly

                    HELEN (laughing)
        Hey, that's a great idea. Chris and Billy
        Asked me the same thing last night. We
        Can make it a foursome.

                    ZIGGY
        That's not exactly what I had in mind.

                    HELEN
        I didn't think so. My mother warned
        Me about boys like you.
(Then, with a look towards Pete)
        Thanks Pete. The coffee was great
        the lesson wonderful.

Then with another look to Ziggy

                    HELEN
        Come on. We got work to do

And she heads for the studio with Ziggy following behind.

INT   CONTROL ROOM CU PETE
      A smile and a shake of the head as he watches them go.

INT   HALL ELEVATOR DOOR OPENS
      Benny Goodman, followed by Band Boy carrying clarinet case, steps out

INT. MLS RECORDING STUDIO
      The Goodman Orchestra seated behind music stands. Helen standing at a microphone behind a sound baffle. Goodman walks in, looks around then goes behind baffle opposite Helen, takes clarinet from band boy, runs a few tune up ripples then, looking towards control room window

                    BENNY (to microphone)
        Okay pops. Let's go.

Unforgettable Helen WGA 1867742   Phillips Wylly

INT. CONTROL ROOM THROUGH WINDOW BETWEEN.
    Chief engineer waves back at Benny. Signals Pete to start turntable on which disk is resting then holds his hand up, fingers extended as he counts down: five, four, three , two, one. And points to Benny.

INT. RECORDING STUDIO. MS BENNY GIVES DOWNBEAT AND BAND STARTS PLAYING "PERFIDIA."
    Written by Mexican Composer Alberto Damingo "Perfidi" (Spanish for "Perfidy") With English lyrics by Milton Leeds, "PERFIDIA" was to become one of Helen Forrest/Benny Goodman biggest hits

INT. STUDIO. CU HELEN STARTS TO SING

INT. CONTROL ROOM MCU PETE DUSTING THE DISK
    As we hear Helen's vocal.
;
INT. DAY. MUSIC STORE MCU PHONOGRAPH PLAYING COLUMBIA LABEL 78 RECORD "PERFIDIA"
    Helen's voice over as camera pulls back to reveal store counter where young people are lined up buying Helen's recording and cash register ringing up 50 cents.

INT STORE.   CU POSTER ON WALL:

"PERFIDIA"
"BENNY GOODMAN/HELEN FORREST
BILLBOARD #1 FIVE WEEKS"

DISSOLVE:

MONTAGE: Short segments of: Goodman/Forrest   Music Over

    KIDS DANCING TO JUKE BOX IN ICE CREAM SHOP :
        "Taking A Chance On Love"
    RADIO PLAYING TO YOUNG COUPLE:
        "It Never Entered My Mind"

TEEN AGE BOY LISTENING TO RADIO
"I'm Nobody's Baby."

INT. MLS HOTEL RESTAURANT
Camera slowly zooms in on table where Helen and several band members are eating breakfast, chatting, enjoying each other's company when Benny arrives. A waitress carrying his breakfast follows him. All conversation dries up as Benny sits, ignores everyone, reads his newspaper and eats.

INT. RESTAURANT MS HELEN AND OTHERS.
Everyone looks a bit strained.

INT. RESTAURANT MCU HELEN as she tries to pick up the pre Benny conversation

HELEN (to someone at table)
...So, did you catch any fish?

MUSICIAN
(He seems a bit uncomfortable)
Ah no. Not a damn one.

INT RESTAURANT MCU. BENNY GOODMAN
Goodman gulps his last bite of food, drains his coffee cup, picks up his paper and without speaking to anyone walks away leaving his check behind.

INT RESTAURANT MS TABLE
Helen and group watch Benny leave. Pan to Helen and move in

HELEN
Son of a gun ! He sits down, Never says a word.
Gulps his breakfast and leaves his bill for us to pay.
Ohhh. That man! Not once in all the time I've worked for him has he called me by my name. Always "pops." Well I've had enough. I'm walkin'.

Unforgettable Helen WGA 1867742   Phillips Wylly

INT.   RESTAURANT MLS BENNY HEADED FOR DOOR AS
         HELEN HURRIES UP TO HIM.

                        HELEN
                  Pops. Hey Pops.

INT.   RESTAURANT   MCU BENNY TURNS TO HELEN.

                        HELEN
                  You forgot this, Pops.
                  (She hands bill to Benny)
                        You're the greatest musician in
                        World and you got the greatest band
                        in the world but you're the last person
                        I wanna work for. I'm through.
                        Good bye Pops…

         (she starts away, then over her shoulder)

                        HELEN
                  My name's Helen, by the way.
                  I kind-a forgot yours, Pops.

         And away she goes.

FLIP FRAME TO INT. ANOTHER RESTAURANT
         Late breakfast time, only half the tables are busy. Camera
         slowly moves in on couple obviously intent on each other.

INT. RESTAURANT   MS ENTRANCE DESK
         Waiter and Host looking in direction of the couple

                        WAITER
                  Where does he find 'em?

                        HOST
                  Damned if I know. (after a moment)
                  This one's not as pretty as yesterdays though.

                        WAITER
              Maybe not. But did you see those boobs.

The conversation is interrupted by a ringing phone. Host turns to take call and waiter turns his attention back to the couple.

INT. RESTAURANT MCU THE COUPLE.
They are obviously interested only in each other

                         MAN
              You haven't eaten very much

                         GIRL
              I guess I'm just too happy to be hungry

                         MAN
              How 'bout some more coffee?

He turns to signal waiter but it isn't necessary. Waiter is approaching with a telephone in hand.

                         WAITER (as he reaches table)
              Mr. James, there's a call for you.
              It's from Helen Forrest. Richard thought
              You might want to take it...

                         HARRY JAMES (He looks to the girl)
              Oh my... Helen...
              (He reaches out and takes girl's hand)
              I probably should take this.
              Would you Mind?

                         GIRL
              No, no. Of course not.

                    HARRY (as he squeezes her hand)
                Okay. Thank you,
            (He turns to waiter)
                Bring the lady a fresh cup of coffee please..

INT.   RESTAURANT CU HARRY JAMES TURNS BACK TO PHONE

                    HARRY
                Helen, hello. How are you?
            (pause as he listens)
                Yeah, me alright. But how did you find me?
            (another pause. Then a laugh)
                I'll remember that.

INT.   HOTEL ROOM CU HELEN ON PHONE

                    HELEN
                (also laughing) Well the same little bird
                Told me you might need a vocalist.

INT. RESTAURANT - CU HARRY

                    HARRY JAMES
                We got a great one. Dick Haymes

INT   HOTEL ROOM   CU   HELEN

                    HELEN
                Yes, but it's time you have a girl too.
                Someone he can sing with.

CU   HARRY
                    HARRY
                Not sure Dick would agree but an
                Interesting idea. Got anyone in mind?

Unforgettable Helen WGA 1867742   Phillips Wylly

INT. CU HELEN ON PHONE

                HELEN
      I bet you can guess. I've had it with Benny

INT   BACK TO HARRY
                HARRY
        I can understand that.
(He thinks for a moment, then)
      Might work, I'll have to clear it with Dick.

INT.   NIGHT LS JAMES BAND ON STAND. CAMERA MOVES IN ON DICK HAYMES AT MIKE SINGING BERT BACHARACH / HAL DAVID HIT SONG "THEY LONG TO BE CLOSE TO YOU."

INT. BALLROOM AS HAYMES BOWS AND STEPS AWAY FROM MIKE AS HELEN STEPS IN TO MIKE TO SING SECOND VERSE.

INT BANDSTAND. MS. HARRY WALKS TO MIKE AND JOINS DICK IN HAPPY APPLAUSE.
   Harry turns to Helen and half whispers

                HARRY
      Guess we gotta give you a job
      Go talk to Bob Malcolm.
      I'll catch you after this set.

INT.   MLS BANDSTAND AS HELEN WALKS OFF STAGE
   Harry and band start another number.

INT.   OFF STAGE AREA
   Where Band Manager Bob Malcolm waits as Helen walks from stage

                BOB Malcolm
      Helen, you were great just like I knew you
      would be. Come on, I got a contract ready
      for you.

Unforgettable Helen WGA 1867742					Phillips Wylly

INT	ANGLE ON HELEN AS SHE TELLS BOB MALCOLM
>	Whoa, Whoa, Bob. No contract 'till I have
>	chance to talk with Harry about a couple
>	of things. I want some special arrangements
>	and I want to sing the whole song, not just the chorus.

>			BOB Malcolm
>	Okay, Okay. Not trying to be pushy.
>	I'm sure Harry will be happy with that.

DISSOLVE INT. NIGHT MCU POSTER IN HOTEL LOBBY

>		"NOW In the GOLD ROOM
>		HARRY JAMES and the ORCHESTRA
>		DICK HAYMES. HELEN FORREST"

INT. GOLD ROOM LS DINNERS, DANCERS AND JAMES ORCHESTRA ON STAGE.
>	Applause as Harry and band play closing theme.

>			HARRY JAMES
>	Thank you. Thank you. 'Till next time
>	On behalf of Helen and Dick and all the Music
>	Makers, let me wish you peace, happiness, and a very
>	good night

INT. OFF STAGE AREA. MLS HELEN HEADED TOWARDS DOOR AS HARRY CATCHES UP TO HER

>			HARRY
>	Hey, hey. Wait up. Where you goin.?

INT CAMERA MOVES IN ON HELEN AND HARRY

>			HELEN
>	No place special. Why?

Unforgettable Helen WGA 1867742   Phillips Wylly

                    HARRY
            Why!? Don't you know what day this is?

                        HELEN (somewhat confused but laughing)
                No. No. Tell me Mister Bones. What day is this?

                    HARRY
            Come with me.

INT. HARRY TAKES HELEN'S HAND AND LEADS HER TO

INT. MLS HOTEL BAR. ROOM IS EMPTY AND BAR TENDER IS JUST TURNING OFF THE LIGHTS AS HARRY, HALF PULLING HELEN, ENTERS.
         Camera moves in as Harry and Helen reach the bar.

                        HARRY (to bar tender)
            Charlie. We need a bottle of champagne

                        BAR TENDER (Charlie0
            Gee Mr. James. We're closed I can't serve anything
            After two o'clock.

                    HARRY
            Yeah, I know. I know.   We just need a bottle
            And some glasses to take to my room.

                    BAR TENDER.
            Okay. Guess I can do that.

INT. HOTEL ELEVATOR
         Harry and Helen, with champagne and glasses enter elevator.

INT. ELEVATOR
                        HARRY (as he pushes floor button)
            You mind if we go to your room? There's
            Always a bunch of kids waiting outside my door.

Unforgettable Helen WGA 1867742   Phillips Wylly

                              HELEN
        (Shaking her head, half in surprise, half in delight and all in fun.)

                   No. I don't mind. Eighth Floor.

INT. HOTEL HALLWAY. MS ELEVATOR DOOR OPENS. HELEN
AND HARRY STEP OUT THEN WALK DOWN HALL TO HELEN'S
DOOR. SHE UNLOCKS DOOR, HARRY PUSHES IT OPEN, STEPS
BACK FOR HER TO ENTER FIRST.

INT. HELEN'S ROOM
        Comfortable, not overly large. An easy chair, a desk and desk chair,
        a large double bed. Harry escorts Helen to the easy chair Then
        opens the champagne, pours two glasses and hands one to her.

                         HELEN (as she takes glass)
                Thank you. Now are you gonna
                Tell me what this is all about?

                         HARRY (In mock surprise)
                You really don't know? Here it is our anniversary
                And you've forgotten.

                         HELEN (In real surprise)
                Our anniversary?

                              HARRY
                It has been one week tonight
                since you joined us Helen.

Unforgettable Helen WGA 1867742　　　　　　　　　　　Phillips Wylly

INT. HOTEL ROOM CU HARRY
Harry clicks his glass against Helen's then takes a sip as he continues

> HARRY
> Helen. That's a lovely name but
> I need something special to call you.
> Something that's just for you and me.

(He takes another sip of champagne)

> HARRY
> And I know what it is. Trees.
> You are my forest and what's a
> forest without trees.

INT. HELEN'S ROOM. CAMERA WIDENS AS HARRY LEANS FORWARD AND LIGHTLY KISSES HELEN. SHE RESPONDS. THE SECOND KISS IS MORE PASSIONATE THAN THE FIRST. THE THIRD KISS MAGICALLY TRANSPORTS THEM TO THE LARGE DOUBLE BED.

SLOW FADE OUT

.INT. DAY. HELEN'S DARK ROOM SUDDENLY BRIGHTENS AS
Fully dressed, Harry steps out of bathroom. Daylight can be seen through closed window blinds as Harry walks to bed where Helen is still asleep. He bends down and lightly kisses he forehead.

> HARRY (a whisper)
> Sleep beautiful Trees. I gotta go do some work.

EXT. NIGHT. MARQUEE CHICAGO THEATER:
"HARRY JAMES ORCHESTRA. HELEN FORREST"

INT. STAGE. HELEN AT MIKE SINGING
HOAGY CHARMICHAEL/JOHNNY MERCER HIT

>Oh skylark
>Have you seen a valley green with spring

INT. ANOTHER STAGE SOMEWHERE HELEN AT MIKE SINGING GENE de PAUL"S

>Oh he's my guy
>I know he'll always be

: EXT. NIGHT. N.Y PARAMOUNT THEATER MARQUEE "HARRY JAMES. HELEN FORREST."

INT. PARAMOUNT THEATER. LS STAGE AS JAMES ORCHESTRA SLOWLY SINKS DOWN OUT OF AUDIENCE VIEW
Closing Theme music fades out as curtain closes.

EXT. NIGHT. PARAMOUNT STAGE DOOR. LOTS OF FANS WAITING AS HELEN AND HARRY EXIT. THEY SIGN AUTOGRAPHS AND MAKE THEIR WAY TO A TAXICAB.

INT. TAXICAB
Helen and Harry get seated then Harry leans forward to tell driver

HARRY
Fifty-second Street.

As taxi pulls away Helen snuggles close to Harry, kisses his ear

HELEN
Thank you for this…You know
We don't have to…

HARRY
You kidding? I wouldn't miss
her for all the tea in China.

Unforgettable Helen WGA 1867742   Phillips Wylly

INT   TAXICAB
Helen kisses him again then the kissing becomes a bit more passionate.

HARRY
I love you Trees

HELEN
And I love you, so much.

EXT. NIGHT CU STREET SIGN 6th AVE/52nd STREET.
Camera pulls back to LONG HIGH SHOT looking south, down 6th Ave as taxi approaches then turns right into 52nd Street where we see many club lights and people walking back and forth across the street. Taxi drives down the street then pulls up.

EXT. NIGHT MS AS PINCUS WALKS TO TAXI AND OPENS DOOR
Pincus, the unofficial doorman for many of the clubs on 52nd Street. Not much over 5 feet tall, heavy set and he knows everyone.
Pincus helps Helen out of cab

PINCUS
Welcome Miss Forrest

HELEN
My god. How do you know me?

PINCUS
Everybody knows who you are
Miss Forrest.

Camera widens to take in Harry who is getting out of other side of cab. Pincus salutes,

PINCUS
You and Mister James. Good evening sir.

EXT. NIGHT ANOTHER ANGLE AS PINCUS ESCORTS HELEN AND HARRY TO CLUB ENTRANCE.
Camera should catch signs indicating the club is "The Three Duces"

Unforgettable Helen WGA 1867742   Phillips Wylly

INT. 3 DUCES. MLS BILLIE HOLIDAY ON STAGE
Camera moves in on Billie as she sings Harry L. Woods hit song

"WHAT A LITTLE MOONLIGHT CAN DO"

As Billie is singing she looks, waves and blows a kiss to

INT. CLUB   ENTRANCE MS HELEN AND HARRY ENTERING

INT. CLUB. MS BILLIE HOLIDAY
As Billie finishes there is applause. She reacts says "thanks" and makes her way to the table where Helen is seated and Harry is waiting to give her a hug.

INT. CLUB MCU   HELEN, HARRY AND BILLIE

                    HARRY (as he hugs Billie)
            You ready to go back on the road?
            Helen can always find another job.

                    BILLIE
            No thanks…

As Helen makes a face at Harry, Billie slides into seat next to her. They hug. Almost tears in both their eyes

                    HELEN
            Oh Billie, it's so good to see you.
            It's been so long….

                    BILLIE
            Yes it has.

                    HELEN
            How's it going.   Things better in New York

> BILLIE
> Better yes. A club like this, we can sit
> together. Use the same toilet but
> There's still 125th Street. South is
> White New York. North is Black Harlem.

> HELEN
> Oh Billie. When's it all gonna stop?

> BILLIE
> Maybe never. Only god knows...
> (Then, brightening,)
> How 'bout chu. You look pretty happy...

Helen brightens too. She breathes on the diamond engagement ring on her finger then proudly glances at Harry as she shows it to Billie.

INT. CLUB MCU BILLIE
Billie takes Helen's hand and looks at ring

> BILLIE
> Oh Helen. It's lovely. Who's the lucky guy?
> Anyone I know?

INT. CLUB MCU HELEN AND HARRY

> HELEN
> No. I don't think so...

INT. CLUB MS HELEN, HARRY AND BILLIE

> BILLIE (to Harry)
> Congratulations Harry. When's the big day?

> HARRY
> Soon as my divorce is final. Probably
> after we get to Hollywood.

                    BILLIE
        Hollywood?   (she looks to Helen)
        That the next stop.

                    HELEN
        Yeah. I guess we're gonna make a movie..

EXT DAY LS CAR PASSING "HOLLYWOOD" SIGN HIGH UP ON HILL IN BACKGROUND.

EXT DAY MLS CAR COMES UP RESIDENTIAL STREET AND PULLS UP IN FRONT OF HOLLYWOOD STYLE THREE STORY APARTMENT BUILDING.

INT. CAR. MCU HELEN AND HARRY

                    HARRY (pointing to building)
        Here we are. What-a-ya think?

                    HELEN
        Looks nice. But we aren't gonna be here together?

                    HARRY
        Oh lovely Trees. You know we can't do that, not yet…

                    HELEN
        So where will you be?

                    HARRY
        I'm supposed to be In a house just up the street
        (He grins and laughs)
        But most of the time I'll be right here with you.
        (He starts to get out of the car.)
        Come on. Lets take a look.

INT DAY INSIDE APARTMENT. MLS AS HELEN AND HARRY ENTER.
They look around. Look into bed room with large double bed

> HARRY
> Here's our room.

(He pulls her close and gives her a kiss. After a moment she pulls away and asks)

> HELEN
> Okay, I like this, but where is your house?

> HARRY
> Come on, I'll show you.

INT. MLS APARTMENT
Harry leads her to a living room window then points to

EXT DAY LS THROUGH WINDOW AT HOUSE UP THE STREET

> HARRY (Voice over)
> That's where I'm supposed to be.

INT APARTMENT. MCU HELEN AND HARRY AS SHE LOOKS OUT WINDOW.

> HELEN
> Gee. That's a mansion. What-a-ya gonna
> do with all that room?

> HARRY
> Well Bob's staying there too and we need some
> room for the guys to come have a drink after
> work. Here in Hollywood everything closes up
> About ten o'clock at night.

(As he is speaking Helen opens the window then starts to climb out on the tiny balcony for a better look.)

Unforgettable Helen WGA 1867742

Phillips Wylly

>   HARRY (in some alarm)
> Wait. Wait. Don't go out there. That balcony doesn't look too safe. You can see the place fine from in here.

INT APARTMENT MS HELEN AND HARRY LOOKING OUT THE WINDOW AT HOUSE UP THE STREET

>   HELEN
> So that is where you will be my love.

>   HARRY
> Where I'm supposed to be…

He turns her around and gestures towards the apartment.

>   HARRY
> So, you like <u>our</u> place?
> (She nods "yes")
> In that case we ought to celebrate. I think Bob put some champagne in the frig'

INT APARTMENT CU WINE GLASS AS CHAMPAGNE POURS IN AND HELEN AND HARRY DRINK
He puts his arms around her'

>   HARRY
> I love you trees, I love you so much.

>   HELEN
> And I love you my darling.

As romance progresses we FADE OUT.

EXT. DAY LS 20th CENTURY FOX SIGN.

EXT. DAY LS STUDIO
Studio is a bustle of activity at 7 o'clock in the morning. Camera moves in to find Helen and Harry as they walk towards stage. Stage is surrounded by Trailers: Star dressing rooms, Makeup, Wardrobe,

EXT. DAY. STUDIO STREET AND STAGE. MS HELEN AND HARRY AS HARRY NODS TOWARDS STAGE ENTRANCE

HARRY
Why don't you grab a beagle, some coffee an' watch 'em rehearse while I go to makeup.

HELEN
Yeah. You do need some makeup after last night.

They separate - Helen heads to stage Harry goes to makeup trailer.

INT. MAKEUP TRAILER
Harry enters and goes to chair where a not too young, not too attractive woman makeup artist awaits him

MAKEUP WOMAN
Good morning Mr. James.

INT. MAKEUP TRAILER MCU HARRY AND WOMAN

HARRY
When a beautiful woman who combs my hair and brushes my cheeks calls me Mister James it makes me feel eighty years old. My name is Harry.

MAKEUP WOMAN (With a smile)
All right, Harry it is.

Unforgettable Helen WGA 1867742   Phillips Wylly

> HARRY
> (As she starts to put protection cloth around him)
> And what is your name my love?

> MAKEUP WOMAN
> Kathleen.

> HARRY (as he takes her hand and kisses it)
> Singing an ever popular song written in 1875 by Thomas P. Wessandorf,

> "I'll Take You Home Again Kathleen."

INT. SOUND STAGE WHERE FILM COMPANY IS GETTING READY TO SHOOT.
THE SET IS HOTEL SHOWROOM AND STAGE WHERE THE STAGE SHOW IS ABOUT TO START.

INT. FILM STAGE DIFFERENT ANGLE MS HELEN
    Coffee in hand, Helen walks away from Craft Service table to a Director's chair with her name printed on the canvas back. Her chair is located in a small semi-circle of similar chairs located behind the camera and the chairs for Director Irving Cummings and his Script Clerk.

INT.   HOTEL SHOWROOM SET   MLS
    Choreographer and stars Betty Grable and John Payne are conferring as Director Cummings watches

> CHOREOGRAPHER
> Okay,
> And he gives count:
> Five...six...seven...eight.

INT.   STAGE MS DIRECTOR CUMMINGS WATCHING AS GRABLE AND PAYNE START DANCE.

Unforgettable Helen WGA 1867742   Phillips Wylly

INT. CU DITTRCTOR CUMMINGS
As he nods approval

                CUMMINGS
    Good. Good. That looks fine
    Shall we try one.

              BETTY GRABLE
    Ready when you are C.B.

INT   STAGE MS DIRECTOR'S CHAIRS
       As Cummings walks to his chair

INT   STAGE MCU ASSISTANT DIRECTOR JOHN POER

             AD JOHN POER
    Okay, Places everybody.

INT   HOTEL STAGE SET.
       Harry James and orchestra ready file into Band Stand

INT   STAGE   MCU BETTY GRABLE
       She waves to Harry as she and John Payne take their places.

INT   STAGE CU HARRY
       Harry waves back.

INT   STAGE MCU HELEN WATCHING INTERACTION BETWEEN HARRY AND BETTY GRABLE.

INT   STAGE MCU DIRECTOR CUMMINGS SEATED. LOOKS TO AD POER

              CUMMINGS
    Alright John, Let's go.

Unforgettable Helen WGA 1867742   Phillips Wylly

INT. STAGE SEVERAL SHOTS AS POER CALLS FOR "QUIET" BELL PLEASE"   AND OTHER ORDERS FROM OTHER PEOPLE: "Speed" "Mark It" etc.

INT. STAGE MCU ASST. CAMERAMAN HOLDING CLAP BOARD WITH TITLE, SCENE AND TAKE NUMBERS

> ASST. CAMERAMAN
> Spring Time in the Rockies
> Scene 23. Take one.

He claps the sticks.

INT. STAGE MCU DIRECTOR CUMMINGS

> CUMMINGS
> Playback…and <u>Action.</u>

INT. STAGE
Several shots as we watch Payne and Grable dance. Harry and band :fake" to playback music. Helen watching.

INT. CAMERA CREW
Operator Running camera. Soundman running playback.   All the stuff that goes on. Then finally.

> CUMMINGS
> Cut! Okay, good. Good.
> Let's do one more.

INT. STAGE MS. GRABLE AND PAYNE
As John and Betty get ready for another "take" she looks to Harry and blows him a kiss.

INT. STAGE MCU HELEN SEES GRABLE - REACTS.

Unforgettable Helen WGA 1867742   Phillips Wylly

INT.   STAGE
We now go into a film making montage as Grable and Payne dance and Helen watches interaction between Grable and Harry. Montage ends as Cummings calls: 'CUT. PRINT."
Poer shouts. 'OKAY EVERYBODY. LUNCH. ONE HOUR."

EXT.   DAY SOUND STAGE, CU RED LIGHT GOES OUT. ZOOM BACK AS STAGE DOOR ROLLS UP ACTORS AND CREW POUR OUT.

EXT   DAY STUDIO   MS HELEN AND HARRY WALKING AWAY FROM STAGE.

                         HELEN
You and Betty Grable seem to be very friendly.

                         HARRY
Oh, what a pain in the ass she is. Thank god we get away from this every night. Thank god for Paladium. Come on, let's get some lunch.

EXT   NIGHT LS PALADIUM BALLROOM LIT SIGN
   "Harry James. Helen Forrest. The Music Makers."
We can hear the James band playing as we read the sign and watch people streaming into building.

DISSOLVE

INT.   PALADIUM BALLROOM. DANCERS AND JAMES BAND ON STAGE
Harry and the band are playing "Shine," an Up Beat number. Dancers…some quite acrobatic, are having a great time.
Helen, seated in front of the piano, is enjoying the music.

INT   STAGE MCU HARRY JAMES
As Harry is playing he seems to be looking and playing towards the right side of the ballroom.

Unforgettable Helen WGA 1867742   Phillips Wylly

INT.   BALLROOM   MCU WOMAN AT TABLE
        Oh my gosh, it's Betty Grable seated at a ringside table.

INT   STAGE MS HARRY JAMES
        Harry lowers his trumpet from his lips and steps to mike

                        HARRY
                Now here's Helen.

INT.   STAGE. MCU HELEN TO MIKE
        As she moves to the mike there is applause but Helen is only aware
        who it is Harry has been playing to. So her lyric seems appropriate
        As she sings Frank Loesser's lyrics to Julie Styne's music

                "I DON'T WANT TO WALK WITHOUT YOU."

INT   STAGE MS FROM BEHIND HELEN SHE FINISHES SONG AN
        ACKNOWLEDGES APPLAUSE
         As Helen moves out of frame camera focuses on two
        spotlights that had been shinning on her.

DISSOLVE:

EXT. NIGHT SPOTLIGHTS ARE REPLACED BY CAR HEADLIGHTS
        Low angle as car passes camera.

EXT.   NIGHT MS CAR PULLS UP IN FRONT OF APARTMENT.

INT.   CAR NIGHT MCU HELEN AND HARRY

                        HARRY
                Hop out honey. Bob Malcolm's got about a hundred
                Contracts for me to sign and I need to read them first.
                It's gonna take me a couple-a hours anyway, so climb
                into bed and get some rest. I'll be there soon..

                        HELEN (obviously unhappy.)
                You have to do that tonight?

Unforgettable Helen WGA 1867742   Phillips Wylly

                        HARRY
        Yeah, I do. I been putting it off and Bob's
        Gonna shoot me if I don't get it done tonight.

                      HELEN (resigned)
        All right…

She starts to climb out of the car but Harry grabs her arm.

                      HARRY
        Give me a kiss.

She complies with a light "peck" but Harry turns it into a more passionate moment.
                      HARRY
        I love you Trees.

                      HELEN (responding)
        I love you too. Now go sign your damn contracts
        And come back soon.

INT   NIGHT CU LOCK ON HELEN'S DOOR
       Helen's hand holding key unlocks door. Camera widens as Helen
       opens door and goes into apartment.

INT   APARTMENT
       It is with a sense of disappointment and annoyance that Helen
       tosses her handbag onto the sofa and heads to the kitchen muttering

                      HELEN
        I need a drink.

INT   KITCHEN
       The refrigerator provides ice cubes. The cabinet above the sink
       provides a glass and a bottle of Scotch.

Unforgettable Helen WGA 1867742   Phillips Wylly

INT   APARTMENT
       Moments later, drink in hand, Helen goes to living room windows
       that provide a look at Harry's house which seems very brightly lit
       up for one-thirty in the morning.

                        HELEN (to herself)
              How many lights does it take to sing contracts?

       She sits down on sofa, sips her drink and turns on radio.

INT.   CU RADIO
                        RADIO ANNOUNCER VOICE
              It's one-thirty in the morning here on Music All Night
              And time for Tommy Dorsey.

       Dorsey music: "In a Sentimental Mood" takes over.

       Helen takes another sip then leans back to enjoy Dorsey's music.
       As music plays softly, Helen's eyes close and camera moves
       to CU Radio

DISSOLVE

INT   APARTMENT CU RADIO a new angle
       As picture dissolves so does music and we are now listening to
        Harry James Orchestra playing "I Don't Want To Walk Without
       You."

                        ANNOUNCER'S VOICE (over music)
              And here she is, Miss Helen Forrest

INT   APARTMENT MCU HELEN
       The announcers voice or perhaps hearing herself coming over radio
       Awakens her.
                        HELEN'S RADIO VOICE SINGING
                     I don't want to walk without"...

       Helen look to wall clock

Unforgettable Helen WGA 1867742   Phillips Wylly

INT.   APARTMENT CU CLOCK SHOWING 2:30

INT.   HELEN STANDS, GOES TO FRONT WINDOW TO LOOK OUT

        HELEN'S RADIO VOICE continues singing

EXT   LS HARRY'S HOUSE FROM HELEN'S POINT OF VIEW
Not so brightly lit up now but still a few lights on

INT   HELEN'S APARTMENT MCU HELEN
She turns away from window and goes to telephone

        HELEN (to phone)
        Harry please. (She listens - then annoyed)

        Well I'll bother him!

With that she slams down the phone, Gathers up her things and heads for the door.

EXT   NIGHT CU FRONT DOOR AND DOORBELL
Helen's right hand presses the bell as left hand bangs on the door.

EXT   NIGHT MS FRONT DOOR
Door opens and a young man looks out, He is the Band Boy. We have probably seen him in background before.

        BAND BOY
        Oh… Miss Forrest. Hi

Not paying much attention to him, Helen pushes her way in

        HELEN
        Where is he? Upstairs?

Unforgettable Helen WGA 1867742   Phillips Wylly

INT.   MS HARRY'S HOUSE ENTRANCE
        Camera follows Helen as she heads for the stairway

                        BAND BOY
                  Miss Forrest...(Then shouting)
                  Helen! Please!!

        Helen ignores him and starts up the stairs

INT   HOUSE NEW ANGLE - HELEN CLIMBING STAIRS AS BOB
        MALCOLM APPEARS;
        Camera moves in on Bob Malcolm as he looks upward towards
        Helen nearing top of stairs

                        BOB Malcolm (softly almost to himself)
                                Jesus!

INT.   BED ROOM DOOR. MS
        Helen does not knock. She pushes door open and looks inside.

INT.   BEDROOM MLS WHAT HELEN SEES
        Harry is pulling on a pair of pants as someone in the bed is trying
        to cover herself. But too late.

INT.   BEDROOM DOORWAY CU HELEN LOOKING

INT.   BEDROOM MCU WHAT HELEN SEES: LADY IN BED

INT.   BEDROOM DOOR. CU HELEN
        Surprise on her face. IT ISN'T Betty Grable, It's Kathleen, the
        Make Up lady.

INT.   BEDROOM - MS HARRY JAMES as he pulls on pants

                        HARRY
                  Trees...Helen...

Unforgettable Helen WGA 1867742   Phillips Wylly

INT.   CU HELEN AT BEDROOM DOOR
        The look on Helen's face says it all. She turns and starts away

INT.   HALL AND BED ROOM DOOR. AS HELEN EXITS SHE
        PULLS DOOR SHUT WITH A LOUD SLAM. AND FILM GOES
        TO B&W

INT.   NOW IN B&W MS HELEN RUSHING DOWN STAIRS AND
        OUT THE FRONT DOOR.

INT.   HOUSE. B&W   MCU BOB MALCOLM WATCHING HER
        GO.
        Obvious concern on Malcolm's face.

EXT   NIGHT B&W LS HIGH ANGLE HELEN RUNNING DOWN
        STREET AWAY FROM CAMERA
        This shot should be same as shot of 16 year old Helen running
        away from Step Father.

INT.   .NIGHT B&W   HELEN'S APARTMENT CU RADIO
        Helen's hit recording of "Perrfidia" is playing. Camera widens as
        With tears streaming down her cheeks, Helen dashes in, runs to the
        doors opening onto the tiny balcony. She pulls doors open and
        climbs out as we hear

                    HELEN'S RECORDING
                For I find you, the love of my life
                    In somebody else's arms'

        EXT   NIGHT B&W BALCONY MS HELEN (Vocal
continues)
        As she look toward Harry's house.

                    HELEN RADIO VOICE
            And now I know my love is not for you.
                And so I take it back with a sigh
            Perfidia's done,   Goodbye!

EXT. NIGHT CU HELEN ON BALCONY
Her eyes reveal the pain she is feeling. Will she jump to end it all?

Suddenly, from somewhere we hear a voice calling

>OFF CAMERA VOICE
>Helen!

Is it Jerome Silverman's voice The voice we remember from days gone by? Then we hear the voice again…perhaps a slightly different voice this time

>OFF CAMERA VOICE
>Helen. Wait…

Helen reacts to the voice. First looking up into the sky, then She looks down.

EXT NIGH B&W MS FROM HELEN'S POV BOB MALCOLM LOOKING UP AT HELEN

>BOB MALCOLM
>Helen. Stay still. Don't move.
>I'll be right there.

Malcolm dashes out of frame as he heads into building

EXT NIGHT B&W MCU HELEN ON BALCONY
She stands there somewhat in shock. Then slowly realizes where she is and carefully backs away from the railing.
A moment later Bob Malcolm leans out the window, grabs her hand and starts to help her back into the living room.

INT MS B&W HELEN'S APARTMENT
As Bob Malcolm helps Helen climb back inside.

Unforgettable Helen   WGA 1867742   Phillips Wylly

INT.   MCU B&W HELEN AND BOB

                    HELEN (a matter of fact voice)
I thought it was real…

                    BOB Malcolm
I know that Helen.   You can't change Harry…
I thought maybe you could but listen, there is a great big world out there waiting for you.

                    HELEN
I know that Bob. And I'm going to find it.

    Camera holds on Helen's face as radio music ends

SLOW FADE OUT THEN BANG!

EXT. NIGHT <u>FULL COLOR</u>. TWINKLING LIGHTS AND LARGE ELECTRIC SIGN
        SANDS HOTEL PRESENTS
          FRANK SINATRA

. Music up - Orchestra and Frank Sinatra ending a number

INT Full Color LS SANDS SHOW ROOM
    Frank Sinatra on stage just finishing song. As audience applauds Camera moves in on Sinatra.

Unforgettable Helen WGA 1867742   Phillips Wylly

INT. FULL COLOR   MCU SINATRA

                SINATRA
          Thank you…Thank you…

He holds his hands up calling for quiet

             SINATRA (continuing)
    When Frank Junior decided he wanted to
    to follow the old man down the singing
    road I told him he'd need to find a style of his
    own and he should listen to a lot of singers.
    I told him there is one I think he should 'specially
    listen to and folks, she's here with us tonight…

INT. FULL COLOR CAMERA WIDENS AS SINATRA CONTINUES

             SINATRA
  (As he points, camera follows direction to table)
     Ladies and gentlemen A big hand for
          Miss Helen Forrest

INT. SHOW ROOM MS HELEN, JEROME, HONEY AND BOB MALCOLM   AS HELEN STANDS TO ACKNOWLEDGE APPLAUSE.

INT. FULL COLOR MCU HONEY AND JEROME
    They smile, at each other as they applaud.

INT. COLOR MCU BOB MALCOLM
    Enthusiastically Bob applauds and makes thumbs up gesture

INT.   FULL COLOR SANDS SHOW ROOM CU HELEN
    Waving, smiling appreciating the applause

SLOWLY THE CAMERA PULLS BACK AND WE SEE
HELEN WAVING, AUDIENCE STANDING AND APPLAUDING

SLOW FADE IN TITLE OVER SCENE

The End

www.ingramcontent.com/pod-product-compliance
Lightning Source LLC
Chambersburg PA
CBHW061457040426
42450CB00008B/1391